"*Carve Your Own Road* is a clear   ......
that will show you the way from a daily grind to an exciting career. Authors Jennifer and Joe Remling know what they're writing about. Both left the security of corporate careers to launch their own careers and to pursue lives they love. Now they're sharing their secrets in this inspirational book.

Pick it up, grab the wheel, and carve your own road to success and fulfillment."

—Lynn A. Robinson, author of
Divine Intuition and *Trust Your Gut*

"Many people feel trapped in a career that no longer makes them happy—maybe it never has—yet each day they feel compelled to continue to follow the herd, as if the traditional path to 'success' is the only road to get there. But just because a road is well trodden doesn't mean it is meant for you. This book will open your eyes to the infinite paths available to travel on in order to find joy in the journey and get to your desired career destination of prosperity and fulfillment. It provides you with a roadmap for how to lay down your own track and make work work for you. When you carve your own road, you find a path along which far greater riches lie than the traditional trappings of success."

—Elizabeth Gordon, author of *The Chic Entrepreneur*

"The Airstream trailer allowed Jennifer and Joe to make their dream of writing a book happen, and that's what Airstream is all about. They were able to travel the country doing interviews, and do it in style. The result: a great read, full of inspirational stories and a roadmap for getting more out of your career while living life to the fullest."

—Bob Wheeler, CEO, Airstream

CARVE YOUR OWN ROAD

Do What You Love and Live the Life You Envision

Jennifer Remling
and
Joe Remling

Your Work. Your Life.
Your Terms.

CAREER
PRESS

Franklin Lakes, NJ

CARVE YOUR OWN ROAD
EDITED BY KARA REYNOLDS
TYPESET BY MICHAEL FITZGIBBON AND KARA REYNOLDS
Cover design by The DesignWorks Group
Printed in the U.S.A.

To order this title, please call toll-free 1-800-CAREER-1 (NJ and Canada: 201-848-0310) to order using VISA or MasterCard, or for further information on books from Career Press.

CAREER
PRESS

The Career Press, Inc., 3 Tice Road, PO Box 687,
Franklin Lakes, NJ 07417
www.careerpress.com

Library of Congress Cataloging-in-Publication Data
Remling, Jennifer.
    Carve your own road : do what you love & live the life you envision / by Jennifer
Remling & Joe Remling.
        p. cm.
        1. Career development—United States. 2. Career changes—United States.
    3. Success in business—United States. I. Remling, Joe. II Title.

HF 5382.5.U5R44 2009
650.1--dc22

2009000031

Acknowledgments

One of the best things about writing this book is the journey we went on and all the wonderful people who helped along the way. We interviewed people about following their dreams, and all those who participated helped us to achieve our dream of writing this book. That's synergy!

Airstream played a big role in helping us launch this project by providing the amazing travel trailer for the Carve Your Own Road journey. Tim Garner and Bob Wheeler at Airstream were key supporters of this project, and we want to express our deepest gratitude and sincerest thanks to them.

We also want to thank all the people we interviewed for this book. Everyone was generous with their time, and were gracious hosts to us while we were on the road. We really appreciate how open people were in sharing their stories with us. We're honored to have met so many inspirational people and new friends along the way.

I want to especially thank my husband, Joe, for his participation in and support of this project. His passion is architecture and design, but he gave of his time, energy, and creativity to be a part of this with me. Being able to do this project with him brought us closer together as we met new people, shared new insights, and dealt with the good, the bad, and the ugly of traveling 5,000 miles towing a travel trailer. He made the experience very special, and one that I will always remember and cherish.

We both have great families who've been with us every step of the way and have given us their support and encouragement. My mom and dad instilled in me a belief that I could do anything, and cheered me on in moments when I felt defeated. When I'm struggling with something, I always think of them and how much they've always believed in me, and that knowledge pushes me forward in difficult times. I have a strong sense of myself, and I attribute that to my upbringing and the supportive environment I had, where I could fail and know that I was still loved no matter what. That type of environment is the perfect foundation from which to explore what's possible and to have the courage to step out there and reach for the stars.

Contents

Part II: The Mindset of Clarity Process

Introduction

I'm not a camper or a backpacker. I prefer to stay in a W Hotel or a nice boutique hotel. My husband, Joe, however, loves going camping and being in the great outdoors. I also love the great outdoors—I just don't want to sleep or shower in it.

We went backpacking for the weekend with a group of friends—once. I definitely checked that off my list. The group we were with laughed at me when we stopped for a snack break midway through the first day, when I broke out some brie, crackers, grapes, and a mini bottle of wine. They all thought I was crazy, but I know they secretly wished they could have brie and crackers instead of trail mix.

Joe and I both knew we wanted more freedom to determine how and where we work. So, several years ago, Joe resigned his position as a principal architect with a large corporate architecture firm in Atlanta to start his own firm with three other partners. Then, I followed in his footsteps by starting my own consulting business. This gave us an opportunity to explore some new freedom and figure out how to incorporate our love for travel with staying connected to our work.

Joe came up with a plan to purchase an Airstream International travel trailer for us to go see the United States as a good compromise between tents and hotels. He figured this would be a great way to get me out on the open road. The Airstream International's interior is like a mini W Hotel room, so I was happy with this idea. It has a nice kitchen, a bathroom with a shower, a sectional sofa, and a flat panel TV—just the way I like to camp!

As we more fully developed our plan to reinvent how and where we would work from the Airstream, the more excited we got about it. We shared our plans with friends and business associates, and we were amazed at the response. Almost without exception the response was, "Wow, I wish I could do that!" But most people felt that it just wasn't realistic or possible because of their jobs and other commitments.

Joe and I have had many dinner conversations about how the world of work has changed dramatically. With the advent of technology it seems that people feel more stressed than ever, rather than using technology in a way to free themselves. The cool thing about the BlackBerry, or, as we lovingly call it, "CrackBerry," is that it gives you the opportunity to be anywhere and still get your e-mail and respond to it.

The problem is, people now sit at dinner with their loved ones while reading and responding to e-mail rather than enjoying food and conversation. Then they become more stressed from reading e-mail and thinking about the work that needs to get done. Many people don't have down time anymore, and they are letting technology control them. The use of BlackBerrys and handhelds has also increased the immediacy of response people expect.

Joe and I decided to determine how to make technology serve *us*. We set out to figure out the best way to use mobile technology from the road—in essence, using technology to free us from having to be in the office all the time in order to get work done.

As we looked at how most people feel about their work, we realized that there is a deep longing for people to have more freedom and creativity in what they do. The surveys I've read show job satisfaction at around 20 percent in the United States. Many people would love to change careers or strike out on their own, but they don't feel that it is possible or realistic in many cases.

We decided to use our adventure in the Airstream as a way to interview people all over the country who are living their dreams and who have figured out a way to change careers midstream or strike out on their own successfully. *Carve Your Own Road* will show how to go about doing this in a way that is realistic and doable.

My career has been focused on corporate recruiting for more than a decade, and I have interviewed thousands of people. I've interviewed people from all walks of life, from entry-level college students to CEOs. What I've noticed is that the majority of people are not connected to what they do. Most feel that they have to do what they are doing in order to make ends meet. We make certain choices and have financial commitments that make it seem unrealistic, if not impossible, to pursue our dreams or passions.

I've also interviewed people who are energetic and connected to what they do, and I thoroughly enjoy those interviews, but they are few and far between. The feeling I get from 80 percent of people is one of quiet desperation. I know that people can have much more control over their experience, but they just don't believe they can.

We set out to find people who are living their dreams and show how they've done it. The focus is on people who were entrenched in a corporate career and figured out how to make a course correction. These are people from all walks of life, backgrounds, and education levels.

Carve Your Own Road has a dual purpose. As we traveled throughout the United States to interview people who are in different phases of living their dreams, we figured out how to reinvent how and where we worked using technology and other tools. We'll share our insights and what we learned from our experiences.

The book also includes a narrative of our story of starting our own businesses and our experiences on the road. We will weave in the interviews and nuggets of wisdom from the people we interviewed throughout the book. There are detailed instructions for how to carve your own road and get in the right mindset for reaching your destination. There is no magic pill or quick-fix solution, but there are ways to do this that are not difficult, and the process can be a lot of fun.

Essentially, *Carve Your Own Road* is the simple idea that we owe it to ourselves, our friends, and our community to live big, to always question the idea of success, and keep those things that are important to each of us in focus. Many of us have lost our focus and are in career situations that are no longer serving us. This book is about taking back the control of your life in order to live and work on your own terms, creating your own definition of success.

PART I:

THE JOURNEY

Chapter 1

The American Dream: Has It Evolved?

The reasonable man adapts himself to the world; the unreasonable one persists in trying to adapt the world to himself. Therefore all progress depends on the unreasonable man.
—George Bernard Shaw

Everyone talks about the American Dream. What is it? The definition varies depending on whom you're talking to. Immigrants once came to America in search of more opportunity and prosperity and to escape oppression just as our founding fathers did. Today, immigrants still come to America for these reasons, and America is still one of the best places on the planet to achieve your dreams.

However, I think for many of us who grew up in America, the American Dream simply means going to college, having a family, owning a home, having a successful job or business, and having the ability to buy and own what you want. These are good goals and pursuits, but once they're realized, if you don't continually focus on what will make you happy—other than things or titles or money—you will likely find yourself feeling unfulfilled and stuck.

15

Many people follow the prescribed path: going to school, getting a professional job and a home, and having children. Such a path requires that we make decisions about our future while we're in school, with very little view into the professional world and what those roles are really like. We're encouraged to major in subjects that will "pay well" or are paths our parents think we should take, with little regard for our real talents and passions.

Things have changed dramatically in the last 25 years, and many times this prescription leads us to feeling unfulfilled and stressed out. The problem is focusing primarily on external things and status rather than finding out what will *really* make us happy. It's very difficult to break this cycle once you're in it; we're a country of consumers, and many of us are bound financially by mortgages, family obligations, and credit card debt.

Once you've met your needs and have the house, the job, and all the trappings of success, if you aren't doing something you're passionate about, you may find yourself acquiring more *stuff* to make you happy, and then you'll realize that there isn't enough stuff in the world to fill that void. What happens is that when all of our basic needs are met, we start looking for fulfillment and meaning in what we're doing. It's normal at that point to start asking yourself the bigger questions in life, such as:

- Why am I here?
- What's the point of my life?
- Do I have a purpose on this planet other than what I'm doing right now?
- How do I find meaning in what I'm doing?

When you start asking yourself these questions, they lead you to think you may need to make some changes in your life, and, let's face it: It's scary to make a big change. Especially when you don't *have* to. Your life is going along nicely, and you think you *should* be happy because you have the things that society says will *make* you happy. You ask yourself, *What's wrong with me? I have everything I ever wanted...I should be happy!*

I remember hitting my goals and thinking, *Is this all there is? Certainly, this isn't it?!* It made me feel empty to realize that the VP title, the salary, and the perks really weren't all that great after all. It was satisfying to reach the goal, but after that it held no real value for me. I wasn't fulfilled by my work; in fact, I was working more than ever and under much more pressure to perform. But when you've spent years in one direction, it's hard to make a course correction. It's like an aircraft carrier trying to make a U-turn!

Many people feel afraid to make necessary changes toward growth because they feel psychological or economical roadblocks. When you've been in a career or job for a long time, it's difficult to even contemplate what it would take to extract yourself from it. The forward momentum is so strong that it's hard to put on the brakes and slow down in order to discover a new route.

Some people don't get to choose when they want to slow down, and are given a "hard stop." Lurline Craig-Burke, whom I interviewed prior to getting the Airstream, is one such person. She got a hard stop when she found out she had an aggressive form of breast cancer at age 37. At the time she was a very successful executive who, ironically, was in the middle of a multi-million-dollar health plan turnaround. She was working long hours and had a lot of forward momentum in her life—in a direction that wasn't necessarily the right path for her. She had also just remarried, blending a family of four children, and had just had a baby. Here's what she said about this time in her life:

> I really didn't have my priorities in order. I was trying to do what I thought was expected of me: get an MBA, have a great job, be a great mother with great children who are excelling—then everything is perfect. I had all the external successes and thought this is the dream; this is what we're supposed to be doing, right? I was working 15-hour days and weekends, drinking a Diet Coke for lunch, and wishing for a 24-hour daycare for executive moms!

> At age 37 I found a lump in my breast and went to the doctor to have it checked out. The radiologist said it was nothing and to come back in three months to have it checked

again. She said she didn't think it was anything and that I didn't need to do anything about it right now. It was strange because I didn't think that I would be at risk for breast cancer at age 37, having never smoked, and not having a history of it in my family. It wasn't even on my radar.

There was something deep inside me that told me I needed it to have it checked out [further]. I kept pushing my doctors until they agreed for me to have a biopsy. When we found out it was one of the most aggressive forms of cancers, every pathology report that came back was always the worst news it could be. Those first couple of days after hearing you have cancer are a living nightmare; it's like a constant hum ringing in your head.

I remember a conversation that was a huge turning point for me. My oncologist gave me a 17 percent chance of surviving the next five years. When she told me that statistic, I felt like I had been punched in the stomach. I picked my head up and looked deeply into her eyes and asked her, "Do you have a 100 percent chance of waking up tomorrow?" She reached for my hand and held it tight, and that day we silently agreed not to talk about statistics again.

I decided to set my life up differently by first setting boundaries at work about my time. I realized that I had been killing myself inside the companies I worked for to build their brand, so eventually I decided to start my own company and create my own brand. I'm no longer defined by money and status; I'm now defined by being true to myself. Learning to surrender has been really freeing, and has opened me up more than I imagined.

I've been 100 percent cancer-free for the last five years. It was a tough road: eight surgeries, eight rounds of chemotherapy, and 36 rounds of radiation. Fast-forward to five years later, and I now have things in my life that are truly great. Less regimen, more flexibility. Less spending, more saving. Less climbing, more walking.

Now, I'm open to all of the exciting possibilities in my life and I'm clear about how to get there. From my experience, I learned that the greatest gift you can give yourself is to surrender. It is the hardest word to hear and an even harder thing to do, but when you do you will open up to amazing journeys you never thought possible, even volunteering at school like all the other moms.

Today, Lurline is living a much happier, more fulfilling life built on her own terms. She now has more time to spend with her family, and she's enjoying being at the bus stop in the afternoons to meet the kids. She said she's enjoying the moment and is also excited about what the future holds because she's creating it one day at a time.

Lurline took her hard stop and turned it into something good for her and her family. Sometimes we're so in the mix of it we can't even see what we're doing to ourselves. The pressure is so great to be successful and to perform well for the company that we get wrapped up in it and lose ourselves in the process.

Dr. Kathleen Hall, whom we interviewed while on the road, is another example of someone who found her way out and is now leading a life that is fulfilled and happy. She worked on Wall Street as a broker in the 1980s when there were very few women in that world. An anxiety attack in an elevator led her to make sweeping changes in her life. She went from being a Wall Street broker to living in the woods, and getting her doctorate in spirituality, and now she runs The Stress Institute, as well as recently launching the Mindful Living Network, an online reality show where she helps people deal with the stresses of life. In her own words:

I was working for a Wall Street firm as a broker. I was successful and had all the trappings, but I hated my life professionally. I was beginning to feel extreme anxiety, and I kept telling myself, "But I've invested all this time and money in education, I can't just walk away from what I've worked so hard to build." I kept negotiating when I was going to leave and how I was going to leave. But then the panic attacks were getting stronger and stronger. I had gotten licensed in everything, and that had taken a lot of time, money, and energy. My practice was successful, and I was good and confident at what I did. I had begun to realize that money wasn't enough and the clients weren't as interesting anymore.

The anxiety grew and I became more and more unhappy. I kept telling myself, "But I've invested all these years in education...." That's why people won't change: because they've put so much into it. But it's really a trap. Then one day I had a full-on panic attack, and I realized I hadn't being paying attention to my stress. I was angry that I'd spent all my time building this practice, making money, and I had a wonderful husband who is a physician, and two beautiful kids, and I pretty much loathed every single part of my life professionally.

At the time, I was reading some of Henry David Thoreau's work, and this quote really struck me: "I went to the woods because I wished to live deliberately, to front only the essential facts of life, and see if I could not learn what it had to teach, and not, when I came to die, discover that I had not lived."

After I read that quote I burst out crying and asked myself, Why am I living my life this way? As I read more about the existential and transcendental movement it caused me to ask myself some really tough questions. I wanted to ferret out what my life meant.

What I've found from very enlightened people is that, instead of running from fear, they danced with it, embracing it. They found there was amazing information in our fears and that it was the path to greatness. I decided to write down the 10 things I was most afraid of. Some of them were being alone, not having status, not being intelligent, or [not] owning a room when I walked into it. I realized I had built a whole life around my fears.

So, I decided to make a big change. I walked away from my job in New York and bought a cabin on 100 acres in the North Georgia mountains an hour outside of Atlanta. I spent a year facing my fears and working on the property, and then decided to go back to school and got a masters in divinity and then a doctorate in spirituality. I have had the pleasure of studying with medical pioneers, including Dr. Dean Ornish of the Preventive Medicine Research Institute and Dr. Herbert Benson at the Harvard Mind/Body Institute, as well as illustrious Nobel Peace Prize recipients including the Dalai Lama, Bishop Desmond Tutu, and President Jimmy Carter.

The prescription for life has become so fixed, we don't even question it anymore. We go through our days blindly following a road carved by others rather than setting out to find our own destinies. Many of us have become stuck in a system that is no longer serving us.

We grow up being told that in order to be successful we must go to school, get a good education, and major in something that will pay us well so we can buy a house and have kids, put money in a 401(K), and retire well. The truth is that this thinking doesn't lead to happiness or fulfillment, and who knows if we'll live to retirement age anyway?

The following passage is from Paulo Coehlo's book *The Zahir*. I think it illustrates what many people fall into and have a hard time getting out of.

You'll grow only half as much as you could have grown, and certainly not as much as you would have liked to. At a certain point, your life will begin to decline, you got halfway, but not all the way, you are half-happy and half-sad, neither frustrated nor fulfilled. You're neither cold nor hot, you're lukewarm, and as an evangelist in some holy book says: "Lukewarm things are not pleasing to the palate."

This is what I was trying to avoid when I set out on my journey and what I think many people hope to avoid. I woke up one day realizing that if I stayed on the path I was on I would be only halfway there, not really experiencing life to the fullest and exploring possibilities for what my life could be. I didn't want to wake up one day and realize I had given up on my dreams and not lived full-out.

I hope to die completely worn out from giving life everything I have and experiencing as much as possible on as many levels as I can find. My dad once told me, "Life is worth living." I totally agree, but for me it has to be on my own terms.

Many people choose their majors in college because their parents or friends thought it would be a good way to make a living, rather than because it was something they were passionate about or had talent for. They then graduate from college and go out into the world to get a job that often isn't what they thought it would be.

I've talked to a lot of 20-somethings recently who are absolutely appalled by the way most people work. They say, "I can't believe people go to this office and sit in a gray cube all day on a computer, and then sit in traffic for an hour to get home." It really is appalling, and it's completely against our nature. Once I stepped outside of my corporate job I felt a guilty freedom that was amazing and weird at the same time. Why did I feel guilty? I know I'm not alone in this feeling. I had been trained to work during the same hours every day and to feel that the entire day needed to be spent on work. Why is that? Who came up with that plan?

We're brought up with a work ethic that just isn't sustainable or life-giving. It's downright unhealthy. When I was working for corporations, I felt that I needed to be available 24/7 and answer e-mail up until midnight if I was going to be like my counterparts and succeed. I remember staying late at the office because my counterparts were staying late, and if I wanted to be viewed as a high performer I felt I must also stay, even if I didn't have anything pressing to do. That's just plain crazy!

Living this way is not carving your own road; it's following the path that was laid by others and is no longer working. In fact, it's crumbling beneath our feet. It's time to make a change, not only for us but also for our children and grandchildren. It's time to set the example for how to live a fulfilling, happy life, while making a living *and* doing something meaningful.

Carving your own road is about creating a path that is uniquely yours; if you choose this path, your life will be rich with expansion and possibility, intense emotions, and experiences. What this means is working and living your life on your own terms. Yes, it is possible! During the course of research for this book, we met many people who have done this successfully and are continuing to do so.

You don't have to become an entrepreneur and start your own company; you can find a way to create your terms inside the corporate structure as well. We have talked to people from all walks of life who found out how to live and work on their own terms in varying degrees and circumstances.

It's time for us to stand up and take our lives back, to make choices that serve us and our families in order to live in a way that is inspired and meaningful. We need to set new examples for how to live with the technology that is available to us and create a way to integrate our desires and dreams with our work.

We've found that people who live their lives this way are happier and much more excited about what is going on around them. It's definitely not an easy path, but it is much more fulfilling. Living and working on your own terms is a constant balancing act and a continual evolution and expansion of who you are. If you choose to live this way, you will experience life to the fullest. Every day won't be perfect, but you will feel more alive than you've ever felt.

What Does Living and Working on Your Own Terms Mean? The Table 39 Accord

Shortly after the idea for this book was conceived, Joe I and went to dinner at one of our favorite restaurants in Atlanta, called Feast. We were seated at our favorite table in the corner, Table 39. We were having a great dinner and started to define what we were embarking on and what this project meant to us. At the time, we had coined the project "Operation Freedom."

We were having a discussion about what freedom meant to us. We had been having many conversations about how wrapped up in our work we had been in the past and the impact it had had on our lives.

Joe had been an architect for a large architecture firm, and was driven to do great work. The culture at that firm, as in many architecture firms, requires you to work long hours in order to work on the good projects and to be respected by the leadership of the firm. Working long hours is a rite of passage for most architects; it starts in college, where they pull all-nighters working on a project or thesis, and continues on into their professional lives.

For the first nine years of our marriage, Joe worked extremely long hours and weekends, and he was successful, regularly getting promotions and accolades. On Saturday mornings he arose just as he did on Mondays to get to the office. I teased him that he was like the Dunkin' Donuts commercial in which the guy would roll out of bed half-asleep and say, "Time to make the donuts...." He was at a point at which he felt compelled to be at work all the time because he believed that was what was required of him to be successful. In truth, if he wanted to be successful at that firm, it *was* a requirement.

I was not immune to the pull of corporate success either. My goals were clearly about climbing the corporate ladder to status and money, thinking that would make me happy. During those years I had shut myself off to really living my life, and I was so focused and stressed out by work that there was little I could enjoy. Joe also teased me and called me "1999 Jennifer" during those years. In 1999, he had told me once that I needed to have a hobby or something as a release, and I jumped all over him, telling him he didn't know what he was talking about. I guess he it a nerve! In 1999, I was at the height of being the corporate bitch, clawing my way up the ladder and trying to skip rungs. I'm still not sure why, or what was driving me. I was just certain that this was what I was "supposed" to do.

So, as we were discussing this at dinner and reflecting on our professional lives and being the "Dunkin Donuts Guy" and "1999 Jennifer," we wrote down on a cocktail napkin what this meant to us:

What is this project about? Freedom. It's about living a life today that is yours. Freedom occurs whenever you choose; it happens every morning on the drive to work, while you're at work, and every evening at dinner—we are all free to be and do what we truly enjoy.

Freedom is:

- Doing what you want; not being at work, but "being" your work.
- Not living for retirement but living every day doing what you love.
- Creating a reality that is your own, not dictated by other people telling you what is real.
- A productive connection to your work from anywhere, allowing inspiration to happen without the constraint of a 9-to-5.
- Contagious.
- Craved by all of us.
- Achievable.

Freedom to think leads to incredible productivity, creativity, and success that is hard to achieve while at "work."

It seems to me that many of us have lost our way, and we're not living an American Dream. "Life, liberty, and the pursuit of happiness" is one of the most famous phrases in the Declaration of Independence. We've gotten pretty far away from that in the last 25 years. It seems many of us have been mostly focused on achieving material success first, and hoping that this will lead to happiness. It doesn't work that way; material success doesn't lead to happiness. It might lead to short-term contentment, but not in any real meaningful sense.

When you get a new car, you're very excited and happy for a few weeks, and then it wears off and you start looking for something new in order to fill that void, such as a big-screen TV or some expensive shoes—you get the picture. My big thing was planning a trip; when I started to feel empty I would surf the Internet for hours planning a trip to look forward to and fill that empty void.

However, I should mention that I'm incredibly grateful for my corporate experience and believe that corporations play a significant role in the economy, in innovation and growth, as well as offering tremendous opportunities for people. What I'm talking about here is not about bashing corporations; it's about us not allowing the job or career to take over our lives any longer. It's about being able to pursue your happiness and dreams on your own terms and to live a full life today, not waiting for retirement. It's about being mindful and intentional about what you want to do and setting boundaries at work in order to do it.

The key is deciding what you want, getting incredible clarity about it, and pursuing it with vigor. You can achieve what you want within a corporate structure, by starting your own company, or by changing careers. It's completely up to you! There are stories of people throughout this book just like you and me who are in pursuit of their dreams and are living fulfilling lives right now. They've taken the leap to being in control of their destinies and owning their choices just as Joe and I did a few years ago.

To me, living and working on your own terms is what the American Dream is about. We live in a country where opportunities abound, and we really can be, do, or have anything we want. It's a shame to let that go to waste! What we've found from the numerous people we interviewed and from our own personal experiences is that when happiness and fulfillment are the pursuit, rather than material success or status, the rest of it falls into place. You may have to make some short-term sacrifices, but it's worth it!

The Physiological Reason for Finding Career Happiness

The workplace is a big contributor to sustained stress these days, with the pace of change, new technology, and the boundaries between work and life becoming blurred. Stress-related diseases and deaths are on the rise, and it's more important than ever to evaluate what you're doing and the effect it has on you.

Stress can cause health problems when a person is faced with continuous challenges without relief. This type of stress can lead to physical symptoms and disease. There are many things at work that can contribute to this type of prolonged stress:

- Disliking your work and working for a difficult boss whom you can't please no matter what you do.
- Fear of losing your job due to a merger, acquisition, or downsizing.
- Inability to have boundaries between work and family, putting pressure on your relationships.
- Pressure to earn a certain income in order to make ends meet even though you don't enjoy what you're doing; the feeling of being stuck.
- Continuous pressure to perform without any time for relaxation.
- Knowing that there is work you could be doing that is meaningful, but can't see how you can pursue it, so you have a constant feeling of frustration.

According to WebMD:

- 43 percent of all adults suffer adverse health effects from stress.
- 75 to 90 percent of all doctor's office visits are for stress-related ailments and complaints.
- Stress can play a part in problems such as headaches, high blood pressure, heart problems, diabetes, skin conditions, asthma, or arthritis, in addition to depression and anxiety.
- The Occupational Safety and Health Administration (OSHA) declared stress a hazard of the workplace.
- Stress costs American industry more than $300 billion annually.
- The lifetime prevalence of an emotional disorder is more than 50 percent, often due to chronic, untreated stress reactions.

When you stay in a prolonged state of stress, your body will continuously secrete stress hormones. At this point, the body begins to experience stress with an extra burden due to the side effects of the persistently high stress hormones. You might exhibit some of these symptoms or conditions:

- Chronic headache.
- Mood swings.
- Anxiety disorder.
- Substance abuse.
- Memory disturbances.
- Heart attack due increased blood pressure, sugar, and cholesterol.
- Stroke due to similar reasons.
- Weight loss.
- Exacerbation of allergies including asthma.
- Irritable Bowel Syndrome.
- Crohn's disease.
- Decreased sexual drive.
- Sleeplessness.

Sounds like fun, huh? I noticed that when I made the changes in my life to being focused on doing what I wanted to do and having a schedule that was more reasonable, my health issues disappeared. Many of the things I struggled with quite literally went away overnight. I had no idea that the symptoms and conditions I was experiencing were stress-related until they disappeared in my new lifestyle.

We spend most of our waking life at work or thinking about work. This presents a big problem when we're unhappy with what we're doing, and we feel stuck. The key is, you don't *have* to be stuck, and we will lay out a roadmap for making gradual changes in your life in order to live and work on your own terms!

Chapter 2

Detours and Dead-Ends

Adversity is like a strong wind. It tears away from us all but the things that cannot be torn, so that we see ourselves as we really are.

—Arthur Golden

For me, getting clarity was a road full of many detours and dead-ends because I didn't take the time to think about it deeply. I had a scattered approach to my life, and the results I got were equally so. My journey toward clarity was a rough one, but worth it.

In October 2000, I took what I thought was a dream position in London. I had always dreamed of living and working in Europe. A company based in San Francisco was opening an office there and asked me to go over and head up the recruiting function. I had been out of college for five years and was thrilled about such an opportunity. Joe and I had just recently returned from a trip to Italy with family and friends where we had been discussing how cool it would be to actually get a job and live in Europe, so the timing was pretty amazing!

What I didn't realize at the time was that the experience of going to London would dramatically change the course of my life, causing me to feel as though I'd lost my identity, and rock the very foundation on which my life was built. It would end up being the catalyst for major change within me.

On my first day at the office in Europe I was introduced to the VP; it was also his first day. The first thing he said to me was, "Who hired you? Why did they hire an American for this role without consulting me?" I'm thinking, *Are you kidding me?* Needless to say, this was an unsettling beginning to my dream job in Europe...and foreshadowed the events to come.

After being in London for two weeks, my boss in the United States resigned, then his boss resigned, and then the entire recruiting group was fired. There I was, in London, my husband had not even arrived yet, and I was concerned about being laid off. He had resigned from a great position in a large architecture firm in Atlanta to come with me. I remember sitting in my hotel room alone, crying, and feeling completely out of control. Control was something I cherished at that time in my life, and losing it was the first step for transformational change in me. I remember talking to my mother through tears trying to explain how I felt; I doubt she understood a word I said.

After Joe arrived, it was a volatile time for both of us. We loved living in London and exploring Europe, but there was a lot of uncertainty that put pressure on us. I ended up working there for about seven months and then laying off the entire team when we closed down the office. I was also laid off because they didn't have a position for me in the United States. This was during the dot-com bust, and layoffs were happening everywhere.

Meanwhile, Joe had gotten a job with a global architecture firm in London and had just gotten settled in. I had urged him to take some time off when he got to London because he had been working so many long hours and weekends for the last few years. (As a funny side note, Joe took his time off very seriously. I remember arriving home one afternoon from work and finding Joe in a bubble bath with a candle, reading a book, with a three-olive martini in the other hand. That image is forever etched into my memory!)

Because Joe was working on the back end of my visa, we couldn't stay in London. His firm offered him a job in San Francisco after I got laid off, so we got an apartment in San Francisco, shipped our furniture, and headed back to Atlanta to wrap up loose ends. The day before we were to move to San Francisco, Joe's company called and told him he no longer had the job because they had lost two major clients and they were laying off people or sending them to the London office where there was work!

Neither of us had a network or many contacts in San Francisco, so we immediately made the decision not to go, as we were both unemployed. The economy was in a major downturn and we weren't confident we would be able to find jobs in California.

It took our furniture two months to arrive in Atlanta, and most of it ended up being damaged. The moving truck had holes in it, and apparently it rained most of the way across country—you get the picture. Everything was wet and molded; water actually poured out of the truck when they opened the doors! I was devastated and pissed off after waiting for two months only to get damaged furniture. Looking back, I understand that it was my life that had unraveled, and the destroyed furniture was a physical representation of that.

Right after the furniture debacle, one of our dogs became ill. Dakota was an 85-pound boxer mix full of love and mischief. He was my protector and my sweetheart; I loved him more than I thought possible. Joe gave Dakota to me as a gift right after we started dating; because he was working late hours on his architecture thesis, he wanted me to have a dog to keep me company. It was really sweet, and Dakota was the gift that kept on giving.

He ate 12 pairs of my shoes that I couldn't afford to replace as a college student, but he was so sweet, cute, and loving that I forgave him. I took him wherever I went and felt very connected to him. He grew to be a big part of our lives, and we deeply loved him.

He had a streak of mischief that served to be his undoing. He liked to get into the trash, and would eat anything that was left on the counter. I remember a time when he ate a stick of butter and an entire block of cheese from our kitchen counter. One day, we noticed he had quit eating, and was definitely not feeling well. I knew that if he wasn't eating, something was gravely wrong. We ended up taking him to the emergency clinic because it was Labor Day weekend and our vet was closed. She told us that he had a blockage, and they needed to go in and remove it. She said that it was dental floss, which one of us had apparently left on the bathroom floor, and he ate the entire roll. It is one of the worst things they can eat, apparently, because it wraps around the intestines and does quite a bit of damage. They called the next morning to say he would be okay and we could come and get him in a few days.

After we picked him up a couple of days later I got the feeling that there was still something wrong, that he wasn't healing. We were very connected, and I could tell that something was amiss. I took him to our vet twice that week, telling them that something was wrong. They wouldn't listen to me, they said it was normal for him to not feel well, and he would heal in a few weeks.

I remember being very frustrated because no one would listen to me, even though every instinct was telling me that something was horribly wrong with him. I remember standing on our deck and looking at him and he looked so exhausted and sick. I pulled his face to mine and looked him in the eyes and asked him not to leave me. But instinctively I knew what was happening. Everyone had been telling me everything was going to be okay when it really wasn't.

So, I rushed him to the vet once again. I think they were beginning to think I was a crazy lady. But this time they realized that something was horribly wrong. I was told that his intestines had ruptured and poison was being spread all over his body, and that they needed to do emergency surgery. He died that afternoon, unable to recover from the trauma. My sweetheart was gone, only 7 years old. It felt like such a gut-wrenching waste! Why wouldn't anyone listen to me??

The next morning, I couldn't get out of bed. I was thoroughly depressed and grief-stricken. The last thing I needed right then was to lose my dog. About 9 o'clock that morning Joe called me from the office and asked me to turn the television on because he had heard something was going on in New York, but didn't have a television at the office. I got up to see what was going on and watched the events of September 11 unfold.

I remember sitting in front of the television for three days watching all the horror in NYC and feeling as though the world must be coming to an end. At that point, we didn't know what was next. Everything had shut down and we were all living in a state of fear. I was unemployed, with nothing to do, and it was hard not having anything to focus on but the atrocities.

I was starting to unravel. I felt as though I was being pulled, kicking and screaming, into an abyss. Everything seemed to be going wrong. I was unemployed and fearful of running out of money. The entire country was living in fear that we may be attacked again, and grieving for the loss of the people in NYC as well as the loss of our perceived sense of security. Having so much go wrong in such a short period of time made me feel angry, sad, fearful, and unsure of myself. I didn't know which way was up or down. I had never experienced anything like this in my life; it was a stripping-away of everything I had known and who I thought I was.

I had worked very hard in my career to attain a certain level of position and status in the workplace, and to a certain extent it felt as though it was my identity. I felt as though that identity had been stripped away almost overnight, and I didn't know who I was anymore. At the same time, we as a society were mourning the loss of our identity as a secure country. Everyone felt sad and fearful to a certain extent.

Looking back, I can see that my goals had been empty and my identity was built on a weak foundation. Because I hadn't taken the time to define who I was outside of my career, losing my job was devastating. My career was built on status, title, and compensation, with little regard for who I really was as a person and what brought me real happiness and joy. I had bought into the dream of material success, thinking it would bring me happiness. How wrong I was!

I felt myself in a downward mental spiral much deeper than I had ever experienced. I am generally a positive, upbeat person, but all of these events just piled on each other throughout the previous year, and I felt as though I was starting to lose it. I had the distinct feeling that if I didn't do something soon to regain control of my mental state, it might be lost forever. I didn't know what to do to get it back, but something told me to go to the bookstore and look for something there that might help me.

I had no idea how this experience would reshape my view of the world. The devastating series of events in my life led me to a Borders bookstore on a Wednesday afternoon to seek out a book to help me. The book that spoke to me ended up taking me on a journey that I never imagined, and has likewise led me here to write *this* book and share these experiences with you.

The book that got my attention was called *The Power of the Subconscious Mind* by Dr. Joseph Murphy. The book outlines how powerful our minds really are and how our focus defines our experience. I think I read the book in one day; it was so fascinating to me that I couldn't put it down. On a deep level, I knew it was true, and I realized that my mental state needed some work.

I decided to try the exercises in the book. I had absolutely nothing to lose at that point! One of the exercises was to watch your own mind, and when you notice yourself going into a negative thought pattern, gently move it into a positive direction. At this time, my mindset was mostly negative, so it was interesting to watch.

In the morning I would wake up and have thoughts such as these:

What am I going to do today? Looking for a job in this economy is pointless. We're close to running out of money...what are we going to do if we run out of money? Oh shit! I'm really scared. My life sucks and I don't know what to do. Who is going to hire an ex-director of recruiting when no one is even hiring? What a joke! I feel like crap, can't I just stay in bed? Who cares anyway?

Not very empowering! I didn't even realize what I was thinking about and how damaging it was until I started to monitor my thoughts. Day by day I continued managing my thought processes. I turned the television off and started focusing on getting a job and getting my life back in order. I started visualizing myself signing an offer letter for a new job and driving to work. I defined the qualities of the job I wanted and started to focus on those. I was gaining clarity about what I really wanted, and how it felt when I shifted my focus to that, rather than on my fears and what I didn't want to happen. It was like training for some kind of athletic event—constantly monitoring and tweaking my brain's performance. At the time I wondered if I was even crazier for trying this.

Three weeks after reading the book and doing the exercises every day I got a call about a potential job. A woman for whom I had worked previously had taken a job with a large manufacturing company, and they needed someone to come in and build a recruiting function. She asked me to come and interview for the role, saying it was less pay than I was accustomed to, but it was a job with a stable company. I also considered her a friend, so I felt lucky to have this opportunity. Her name is Jodi Weintraub, and her story is included in the book, in Chapter 14, as someone who made a decision to change her life, and within one year had accomplished what she set out to do. She's remained a big part of my life, and I consider her a good friend as well as a trusted advisor. She made me an offer the next day, and I accepted the position. Immediately, I felt a huge sense of relief after being unemployed for five months.

I was amazed at how different I felt and the results I'd had in such a short time by choosing what to focus on and pulling my mind out of its downward spiral. I had begun to realize that your mind can spiral up or down, it's up to you. I much prefer the upward spiral!

In just a few short weeks my life was looking much brighter. I felt much better, and was getting results in other areas of my life: I began noticing that my interactions with people were much better and I was generally enjoying myself much more on a daily basis. I noticed, for example, that when I went to a restaurant in this frame of mind I always got good service and that people responded to me in a more positive way. When I was at ease and happy, the world around me was at ease and happy. I found that to be interesting, and it made me realize that I actually did have an impact on the world around me. This realization spurred me on to read every book I could find on the topic of how your thoughts impact your experience and ultimately your life. I went through a period of two years in which I read more than 300 books, from the esoteric to the scientific. I knew there was something powerful here, and I wanted to know as much as I could about the subject and the science behind it.

I know this sounds borderline obsessive, but it was something I felt compelled to do. During this time, the economy was in a funk, and so was the country politically (much as it is today!). But I felt better than I had in years because I was applying what I was learning from reading and exploring how we can affect our reality.

The reason I read so many books was that once I started down a certain path, it led me to another book. I explored many topical areas, and attended seminars and conferences.

I am the type of person who won't accept anything at face value. I have to know *why* something works, and the science behind it. There was an aspect of going on faith in my explorations, but I delved into as much science as I could tolerate in order to understand why controlling our thoughts and focusing our attention on what we want is so important. There is, in fact, a lot of scientific research to support it.

During this time I realized that I was done climbing the corporate ladder; I had lost the killer instinct that it takes to be successful in that world. I couldn't play the game anymore and act as though I cared about shareholder value when we were not valuing our employees or customers much of the time. I know that shareholder value is important, but for many of the companies I worked for, it seemed to be the highest priority.

I tended to challenge the status quo and look for ways to treat employees well in order to retain them. I took it personally when someone resigned from the company, and made it my mission to make things better. This is what made me successful—and drove me crazy at the same time. I was taking things personally in business, and they were taking over my life. My frustrations at work carried over to my personal life.

So, I opted out. I didn't feel that I could make the kind of contribution I wanted to make in the world through the corporate structure. I'm grateful for the opportunities I had and know that I wouldn't be able to do what I'm doing today were it not for my corporate experience. But it was a small part of a much broader picture that was just beginning to emerge for me, and I needed to muster the courage to step out of it.

My experiences had humbled me, and I was determined to focus on doing something meaningful with my life. I wasn't sure what that was yet, but I was going to find it.

While working in my corporate position with Jodi, I had explored the idea of becoming an entrepreneur. I knew that I wanted to be on my own, but I wasn't sure how to do it. I was making a nice income, and the thought of not getting a regular paycheck was scary for me. We also didn't have a huge amount of savings set aside to bridge the gap in income for me.

Joe quit his job in 2004 to start his own company with three other partners, so me leaving to start *my* own company was doubly risky. But his success inspired me; it was great to watch him expand who he was and rise to the challenges of running a business. It was fun to watch him grow and do things he had only dreamed of. I decided to apply the information I had learned from all those books to taking my own leap into entrepreneurship. I knew I wanted to write a book, but I also knew that wasn't going to pay the bills. I took another new position with a global consulting company that I thought would be challenging and fulfilling, but after just three months in that role, I realized I couldn't do the corporate thing anymore. It was time. It was imperative that I step out of the corporate world.

I was traveling every other week to Los Angeles and was under a lot of stress to perform feats that weren't realistic with the tools and resources we had. And, worst of all, I didn't care anymore. I didn't care that we needed to hire 300 people in the third quarter to make our numbers; it just didn't matter to me.

For example, the company would double the number of people we needed to hire in a quarter without giving us more budget or resources to do it. I had a team of 12 people that could hire 100 to 125 people per quarter, and they increased that number to 300 and told us we needed to figure out how to do it. We got that notice two weeks before the quarter started. I was tired of being stressed out and having to perform at levels that weren't sustainable.

At the time, I was traveling a lot with a colleague, and we conceived a business idea for a company. We worked on it nights and weekends for a few months. Our idea was an outsourced recruiting company that focused on small, high-growth companies that couldn't afford to have their own full-time team. We tested the idea with some people in my network and got great feedback, so we decided to resign our positions to start the company.

When we resigned, the CEO at the time asked if we would fly to Boston and present our business model to him. He said he was looking for new service lines to offer and was intrigued by what we were doing. We presented it to him, and he asked if we would stay at Sapient and do it there as a business unit reporting directly to him. We went through a few months of negotiation as to what this would look like, and then finally agreed to stay there and do it because it would be a lot les risky—or so we thought.

It was a tough road trying to create a start-up in a large, public company. You don't have the opportunity to be nimble the way you need to be when launching a company. We also had leapfrogged the management team we had reported to in the recruiting organization by reporting to the CEO, and they were not pleased about it. The politics at that company were out of control; it reminded me of a fraternity.

Four months into building our new business unit, the CEO resigned unexpectedly, leaving us without an executive sponsor. We needed support from someone on the executive team, and at the time the company was going through many struggles on several different fronts. The management team was honest with us and said it would be mostly a "distraction" for him at that point to support us. I completely understood his perspective.

During this time frame, I was meeting with a client we were trying to get to sign the Sapient contract. I had worked with this client, Neil Thall, for quite a few years, and he knew me well. Neil is someone for whom I have tremendous respect, and has played a big role in my professional life. He said, "Jennifer, you don't seem happy with this arrangement with your company; why don't we tear up this contract and I sign one with Jennifer Remling, Inc.?"

Driving back to the office that day, I was turning the idea over and over in my mind. All of a sudden I had a vision—actually, two at the same time. On the left side, I saw a series of doors opening into infinity—it was beautiful. On the right side, I saw a dark road with roadblocks, fallen trees, and a storm. It was clear to me that the series of doors opening represented me quitting my job and going out on my own. It was a true leap of faith, but I felt that if I jumped now, the net would appear. And it did.

The deal I signed with Neil didn't cover my income, but it was close. Within 30 days, I had another contract that more than covered my income and also allowed me to hire someone. Then almost immediately after that I got more business, it was amazing how things fell into place! I don't think I had ever had this much luck doing anything in my life. I had finally made the leap from the corporate world into doing my own thing! It was a journey getting there, but it was the best thing I had ever done.

I was up and running, and it was very exciting. I had the mind space once again to focus on my dreams. My dream wasn't starting a recruiting business, but I saw it as a bridge to my dream of writing a book and becoming an author. I had begun creating a process that helped me to make this leap, and it was working quite well.

I had set out on a journey to find myself and to find meaning in my life. I didn't know what I was getting into when I started this, but once you start on this path there is no going back. There have been many twists and turns along the way, and I wouldn't change a thing about it. I feel that all the things that happened needed to happen in some way for me to be where I am today. There were some painful years; there were times when I thought I was going crazy or looking for something I would never find. But I kept at it, and pursued it vigorously, because I knew I couldn't go back to being the person I was.

One morning, I woke up with an idea that would change my life. It is what I call my "Shiny Thing," because I was so excited about it, and was determined to overcome all obstacles and enroll as many people into the project as I could. It is the thing that mobilized me to put a systematic practice into place that would help me achieve my vision. In Chapter 4, I will explain this in detail and how it transformed my life.

Chapter 3

The Marathon Drive for Success

Success is the sum of small efforts, repeated day in and day out.

—Robert Collier

In Joe's Words

Jennifer and I consistently discuss how we became the people we are today and the events that have shaped our perspective and given us the inspiration to carve our own road as adults. Jennifer was born to challenge the status quo. Spend any time with her family and you will be in tears laughing at some of the stories of her escapades in the 1980s alone. Thank God YouTube did not exist when she was 17. From a very young age, Jennifer strongly believed in challenging authority and the constraints that society could quietly place around us all. It is safe to say she didn't share the same perspectives of many of her teachers, and even her parents on a few occasions. As a result, her path has been circuitous, weaving through many opportunities in search of her passion.

For me it was very linear. I did things the "right way." I was the product of a career Army officer and a professional mother. As a kid, I saw them both develop amazing careers. Because both of my parents worked, I was able to form my own agenda as a teenager. I had always focused on being an architect. It was never a choice; from my early memories it seemed to be what I had been born to do.

Jennifer and I hash and re-hash lessons learned over dinners, road trips, and breakfast. We recall our time together in West Texas, how broke we were our first year in Atlanta, and the fear of moving to England. We are continually amazed that everything we experience has a direct connection to our lives as professionals, and as entrepreneurs. We do not lead two lives; the life we lead is a single entity full of success, failures, and dreams.

In one of our many conversations on the subject I pin-pointed exactly when this whole entrepreneur thing started for me and how it has evolved to today. Jennifer and I were in Chicago for the LaSalle Chicago Marathon. Jennifer had come to cheer on myself and a few other friends as we mixed it up with 25,000 people for 26.1 miles. It was an amazing fall day in 1998, one of those days when we would seriously look at those 8 1/2-by-11-inch flyers of kickass apartments (that never really exist) in the corner real estate offices and debate leaving all our belongings in Atlanta and moving to the Loop, or maybe Lincoln Park, or a warehouse loft off the red line. It was a nice day, and the streets were full of people.

For the last five months I had trained diligently for this, my first marathon. It was not as though I was a runner; I actually never really ran for fitness before deciding to take on this challenge. I was fit, but I had no clue what was about to happen to me, not only physically but mentally.

I started the race with a definitive opinion that most marathon runners are insane. I still hold this opinion. Nonetheless, I decided to join the madness and throw myself in. My goals were simple: (1) Finish. (2) If you meet goal 1, beat Oprah's time from 1994 (4:29:15).

Physically, I was in great shape, and I was mentally prepared. I knew that marathons are all about making it to the last six miles.

The first 20 were basically a running tour of Chicago: "Cool, I am running by the Tribune Building!" Once the excitement of it all wears off and your body starts to fight you, the run quickly turns into a series of mental games. I started to talk to myself around Chinatown, at mile 18. It is amazing how singularly focused you can become when you are in this type of situation. Quitting is totally an option. You can stop the pain just by quitting. Why the hell not, right? Not for me. It was too much effort to get that far to quit. For the next four miles I became locked into a rhythm that wouldn't catch up to a retiree on a Rascal Scooter.

I slowly emerged from the shadows on the north end of McCormick Place, the multi-million square foot convention center that sits just south of Grant Park, at mile 25. I was only a few strides into the sunlight when a deranged young man, maybe in his mid-20s, caught my eye and started screaming at me. I was trying to understand what he wanted from me—was he real, or a hallucination brought on by the bright sunlight in my eyes or my complete lack of energy? He was relentless; I think he even mentioned something about my mom....

As I slowly crept by, trying to comprehend it all, placing the man in my mental Rolodex for the afternoon's storytelling that was sure to come, I was overcome by a feeling of complete calm. Through all the yelling and name-calling he struck a chord with me. He woke me up. As my mind cleared, I realized the kid was actually a volunteer at the last drink station before the finish, yelling at me to do my best. That kid knew that each one of us who came out of the tunnel at McCormick Place had almost made it to the finish. He also knew we had no idea how close we were. The last mile after that turn was the fastest mile I ran. He was all about getting us to close the deal, to look up and push to the finish. It was a small moment that would reshape my life.

Two years later I was sitting in a bulkhead seat on a Delta Airlines 777 on my way to meet Jennifer in London, where she had taken a position for a San Francisco–based company, and recalling that fall day. It had been more than 24 months, but the awakening had really just begun. I saw the move to London as an opportunity to explore beyond the traditional boundaries I believed existed for me professionally and personally. It allowed me the freedom to be interested in the world around me again, instead of hammering through the day with my head down as I had for the previous five years as a corporate architect in Atlanta. I was always one to work hard and play hard, but the play was quickly going away, making me a one-dimensional, one-track-minded bore. I was becoming "that guy," the one we despised in school, who used phrases such as "think outside the box" during our project critiques.

To combat this feeling of mediocrity, I determined that I should take some time away from architecture and enjoy London to the fullest. I would know when the time was right to be an architect again. I spent the better part of three months touring through the National Gallery, The Tate Modern, and the Tate Britain room by room, with no schedule, and time to enjoy what I wanted (the beauty of free admission to museums in England). I endlessly walked the city or rode the tube everywhere I could to see the neighborhoods and grand streets I had studied as an architecture student but never really understood until now. It did not take long to fall in love with London and architecture again. Within a couple of months I was refreshed and excited about getting back to the work I enjoyed.

I took a position with a global consulting company as a design architect, and jumped in headfirst, charged up to be back at it. It didn't take long to slip into that traditional driven mindset, unaware of the world and opportunities that were around me—the hard-working bore was back. Everyone goes through this (I think), but the scariest part was that it came too easily. I truly believed that I had to impress those around me at all times; I had to do the impossible; I could not fail; I had to win; I had to be the hero in order to be successful, which I hoped would make me *feel* successful. It was so bad that I turned down a trip to Paris with Jennifer because I had a deadline! I still regret that decision.

After the dot-com bust at the beginning of 2001, Jennifer's company pulled the plug on the London office. Our deal was done and we were headed back to the States. I secured a position in Atlanta with the firm I had left the year before, and jumped into the same studio, which completed my reconstitution back into the daily grind. I was again numb to most things around me and single-mindedly focused on being the hero again. Don't get me wrong, I was very proud of what I had accomplished professionally. It was a textbook "work hard and reap the rewards" type of career. I was 33 years old, a principal at a major architecture firm, and leading the design of the firm's largest commission at the time, the Georgia Aquarium. I was the golden child; I had become the hero I wanted to be, but Jennifer and everything outside the office were paying the price for my success.

Early in 2004 my studio rode the edge of success to deliver a monster aquarium design in less than six months, a design effort that had not been done before. We kept on a torrid pace; 60- to 80-hour weeks were typical for most of the 20 people involved to meet unrealistic deadlines. We were as close to being out of control as a group of young professionals could be in a large corporate firm, but that was the way I wanted it.

I saw this studio as the underdog to some unseen challenger. I wanted to create a culture that was about ownership and passion. I loved watching architects and designers fight over design issues; it showed they cared enough to stick their necks out for what they thought was the right solution. That was what that project and studio was about. *It was what I was about.* The talent in my studio was unquestioned, and the attitude and the will to reach a little further to succeed was an amazing thing to experience. I wanted more of it, and saw my future at our firm being in studios like this. Full of passion, commitment, and a little belligerence—that was the architecture I fell in love with.

At our firm, the aquarium studio's reputation began to take on its own life throughout the entire office. I heard through the grapevine that many of the principals thought we were completely out of control, that our egos had gotten too big. My personal favorite was, "We need to break that party up." Party my ass! I was looking at one of the most successful and talented groups of architects and designers in the firm, working their tails off. But because we all got along, listened to music openly, and laughed as much as we argued, we were labeled "the party." So the senior principal sat me, along with Dan the aquarium project manager and Lucy the lead interior designer in charge of our project, down for a "Come to Jesus" talk.

It was told to us straight: "You should not think that you are special for doing what you did on the aquarium. Anyone in this firm could have done what you did." I found it an interesting statement, and one of the dumbest remarks anyone has ever said. Those who have been involved with a team that has done something impossible, something unexpected, understand the pride and the commitment it takes. It is not something that "anyone" can do. That discussion symbolized the beginning of the end for me. It wasn't that day alone that caused us all to question whether our commitment was to the firm or to ourselves, but it helped to move the discussion along. Dan, Lucy, and I had built something special within the firm, and we knew it.

We understood that our future lay square on our shoulders, and it was up to us to define it in the way we saw fit. I knew that it would be up to me to create a better future for Jennifer and myself by clearly defining how I was going to work from this point forward. I had to redefine for myself what success was and how to fill that need to be a hero by being one at home first. This is still a work in progress.

In June 2004, Lucy, Dan, and I resigned from the firm and launched our firm, ai3, along with Lucy's husband, Patrick. That last year at the firm will always be a defining moment for each one of us, and we will always credit the firm for the opportunities we had, but now it was up to us to create the culture of ownership and success we had there.

When I think about what gave me the guts to resign from a perceived secure future and create a business, I recall that fall day in Chicago when I had blown up completely in my attempt to run a marathon. I honestly compare a lot of the trials I've faced to that day. It's clear to me that I won't leave all my hard work behind, everything I challenged myself to do, in order to fail in the last mile. But I also remember that support worker; I know I can't do it alone. That is what Carve Your Own Road is to me.

Chapter 4

The Shiny Thing

Dreams pass into the reality of action. From the actions stems the dream again; and this interdependence produces the highest form of living.

—Anaïs Nin

What Is a Shiny Thing?

A "Shiny Thing" is something you are so excited about that you feel compelled to take action on it. When you find it, your focus becomes clear and you're able to overcome hurdles, fears, and lack of motivation to achieve it. You can feel that if it came true, it would be a big deal for you—maybe even change your life. I believe that every single one of us has a "Shiny Thing" that is unique to us. Unfortunately, many of us bury our shiny things deep inside of us and forget what they are because we're so busy living and doing.

This is what setting big goals is all about. When you have a big goal and something that is very compelling to you, it's much easier to take action on it, get other people excited about it, and build momentum toward it. Carving your own road is about thinking big, breaking down barriers, and moving way beyond where you've been before. My Shiny Thing ended up being the Airstream and the project of writing this book, and the achievement of it changed the direction of my life.

The Shiny Thing (Jennifer's Version)

The morning I woke up with my Shiny Thing was just a few months after quitting my job and starting my business. Being on my own allowed my juices to flow and enabled me to connect with the creative part of myself. When I was in a job, I gave it everything I had, and at the end of the day I had nothing left for me. My evenings consisted of coming home, having dinner and two glasses of wine, and falling asleep on the sofa or climbing in bed with my laptop so I could stay on top of things.

On this particular morning as I awoke, there was a persistent idea on my mind. It stuck with me, and the more I thought about it, the more excited I got. I had no clue at the time how much this one idea, once acted upon, would change my life!

Joe had been shopping for and wanting to buy an Airstream travel trailer for a few months. Since becoming entrepreneurs and realizing that we owned our schedules, we decided that we wanted to get out more and enjoy life. We both love being in the outdoors, but I'm not into camping. I like my creature comforts, such as Egyptian cotton sheets, plush towels, a refrigerator, and electricity.

I woke up one morning with this clear vision for pairing the Airstream with writing the book. My idea was to get an Airstream and travel around the country to interview people who had decided to make big changes in their careers in order to pursue their dreams. I sat down, wrote out the idea, and presented it to Joe. He told me he liked the idea, but was a little hesitant about how much work it would take. He was fine with me getting Airstream to sponsor us and let us use one of the trailers in order for them to get some good PR.

Upon doing more research on Airstream, it started to unfold as the perfect vehicle for this adventure and project. Their catalog had a quote in it that really struck me: "Today, Airstream is once again the perfect vehicle for chasing dreams, pursuing the moment, and enjoying a broad, expansive vision of life. See More. Do More. Live More."

Pairing an Airstream with this project seemed synergistic to me. In essence, what Joe and I would be embarking on was similar to what Airstream is all about. This was the beginning of something big; I could feel it, and I think Joe could too. The next morning, I got up and wrote an overview of what the "Carve Your Own Road" project was all about. Then, Joe and I worked on it together, and he added to it and put some great graphics and design in place.

Thank goodness for Joe and his creative talent, or this project would never have gotten off the ground. Left to my own devices, I would have only had the ability to put together a boring Microsoft Word document! Joe's creative vision and skills made this idea come to life.

I was so excited at this point; I realized that this was my Shiny Thing. I had finally found what I had been looking for throughout the last five years. I felt so excited and so inspired when I thought of this project and all the possibilities, that I could think of nothing else. I was *focused*, like a laser beam. This type of clarity of purpose had always eluded me somehow, but I had finally found it.

The thought of traveling all over the country with Joe and interviewing really cool people for a book was thrilling to me. The idea of being out of the office and outside my comfort zone, meeting new people, writing a book, and following my dream made me feel totally alive again. I was waking up every morning with a renewed excitement for life.

This excitement led me to doing some research to find out who the CEO and head of marketing were for Airstream. At the time, Tim Garner was the VP of marketing. I found him on Google, my favorite tool. I reached out to him by e-mail and left him a voicemail. After about two weeks, Tim sent me an e-mail inviting me to give him a call. I was so excited! When I got on the phone with Tim, we connected immediately. He's a great guy, and said he could relate to what we were doing, as he had dreamed of going out on his own for a long time and our project really resonated with him.

He told me that he gets quite a few proposals similar to ours every week, and that he'd think about it some more and get back to me. He reached out to me a few weeks later, saying he had some real interest. Tim had been working on an idea to build an Airstream that was focused on businesses, and because Joe was an architect he felt we might be a good fit. Indeed, because our proposal was to live and work from the road in the Airstream, it was the perfect fit.

He asked if Joe could put some plan ideas together with his architecture and design skills for an Airstream that would serve as a work/live model. The current Airstreams are focused on the residential capacity, and he wanted to see a prototype for one that people could live in and work out of at the same time. We got Joe's team together at ai3 one cold January afternoon to brainstorm on this idea. Joe has a great team of people who love this kind of work and looking at all the possibilities. They came up with some really cool ideas, which Joe put on paper and sent to Tim.

Tim was intrigued, and he decided to meet with us when he was in Atlanta for a trade show later in January. We spent an afternoon with him, took him to dinner, and had some really great conversations. I felt as though we had made a new friend; we were all in alignment in our thinking about work, life, and business. (Tim has since left Airstream, but to this day I consider him a friend and a big part of the success of this project.)

This was an exciting time for me, the possibilities were percolating, and I could feel it all coming together, even though I knew we had a long way to go in convincing Airstream to let us use one of their trailers. Our dialogue went on for a few more months with Tim, and finally we were able to set up a meeting with Bob Wheeler, the CEO of Airstream. He thought it would be important for him to meet us and hear our vision in person, so we scheduled a meeting and flew up to Ohio to meet with him.

We created a presentation full of imagery, and detailed what the benefits for Airstream would be in working with us. When Bob Wheeler walked into the conference room that morning he looked closed off, as though he knew he was going to tell us no but he was going to allow us to present the idea anyway. As we went along, I could feel Bob warming to the idea. Toward the end of the meeting he was even giving us some ideas for things we could do. I felt that we had him! We left feeling very good about the meeting and our potential relationship with the company.

A month later, we heard that we were a go! I can't tell you how excited I was at this point. It was an amazing feeling to have conceived of an idea this big and to have it come to fruition. Most of our friends thought we were crazy, and that Airstream would never agree to work with us. I never listened to anyone because I had my Shiny Thing and knew it was going to happen.

Concurrently, while we were working on the deal with Airstream I was working on getting us a literary agent so we could get a book deal. I had heard that I might have to contact more than 50 agents before someone would agree to take us on. So I decided to also focus on finding a great agent who would help us. A friend of mine referred me to an agent by the name of John Willig.

I read John's bio on his Website and was impressed with his background, experience, and connections in the industry. I sent him a book proposal and reached out to him to follow up. He set up a call with us and agreed to take us on! He was the first agent I contacted, and he was perfect. He was excited about the project and saw potential for us to get a publisher.

Things were coming together so quickly, my head was spinning. I was so excited about getting John to take us on; it just felt as though everything was falling into place. I've found that when you're passionate and excited about something, and it's *yours*, you can enroll other people and get them excited as well. This project had that sort of momentum all the way through.

It was during this time that the framework for the Mindset of Clarity process began to emerge. This process is not only a framework for getting clear about what you really want, but also provides the tools and techniques to build momentum and achieve your vision by bringing it to life on a daily basis. Part II of this book is devoted to delving into the details of this process, which is rooted in neuroscience and psychology, and how you can apply it to your life. It reconnects us to our dreams and the expansive world of opportunity beyond. I began using processes I had tried throughout the last few years, putting them together in a systematic way. It was as though the puzzle pieces were coming together to form a clear picture for me. Using this process contributed greatly to the success and the accelerated time frame of our project.

I had read about the impact of visualization and how it can prime you for taking action. Throughout the last few years I had tried it from time to time with some success. When I had this clear picture about what I wanted to create, I decided to use it in a systematic way: I would get up in the morning and write about how I saw my day unfolding, visualizing success with this project, and feeling how it would feel when it all came together.

Specifically, I would write about how we convinced Airstream to work with us; I would "feel" it happening with all of my senses. I felt how it would feel when we got the word that we were a go, how it felt to go to Ohio and pick up the Airstream and drive away with it, how it felt to meet and interview cool people, and how it felt to have my dreams come true. Every single day I did this exercise on a deep, feeling level.

Many aspects of this practice started to emerge, and I learned to put it all together in a meaningful way to keep the momentum going. I realized that it was an organic, evolutionary process that helped me to continually expand my thinking about what was possible, take inspired action, and deal with stress and anxiety as it came up. The Mindset of Clarity process has changed my life in ways I never imagined. This book, in Part II, outlines all the components of this process, how to integrate it into your life, and how the people we interviewed are representative of what it's all about.

I remember the day everything came together in one single moment in time. Joe and I purchased a Nissan Armada so we could tow the Airstream. The Armada had been part of my visualization and focusing process every day. I was leaving the Nissan dealership the day we bought it, driving it home for the first time, knowing that the next week we were leaving to drive to Ohio to pick up the Airstream they had agreed to give us.

All of my emotions came rushing in at once as I realized what had happened. I had been here before many times in my visualization, and now that this was all *actually* happening, I felt a complete sense of awe and gratitude I can hardly explain. It was a moment I will never forget, because I knew at that moment that we really do create our own reality. I had the physical manifestation of my impossible dream to prove it!

Joe's Version

Long before our Carve Your Own Road adventure, on a Thursday afternoon about 3 o'clock, Jennifer and I hit the road, squeaking and banging a well-broken-in rented recreational vehicle with beige fiberglass side panels out of the parking lot at the La France Street lofts in Atlanta, headed to Indianapolis, Indiana, for the United States Grand Prix, one of two Formula One races in North America that year, the other being in Montreal. Catching the race in Montreal would have been way too chic for us—anyone can just buy a plane ticket and fly to Canada, book a nice hotel room, and sip lattes on the plaza. But I wanted to get dirty and see part of the country from the road, in "Go RVing style."

I was raised a road warrior, like many of us who grew up in the late 1970s and early '80s in a middle-class family. My dad was all about hitting the road to visit relatives or major tourist destinations, no matter the distance. Thank God I didn't have some long-lost cousin twice removed from my dad's side living in Alaska! Every road trip had the essentials: one major fight between my sister and I within the car that usually started with a debate over which stitch line in the back seat was the one that established "sides," at least four hours of I Spy, a stop at Stucky's, a missed exit that wasn't noticed for at least 30 miles, and the standard "buckle up, mom's driving" harassment of my mom every time she got behind the wheel.

Road trips taught me a lot about our family, showed me a lot of about our country, and left me with some great memories. It was the fundamental American experience; a small adventure every time. I loved combing over maps with my dad, planning the next day's drive—it was the beginning of my wanderlust, the desire that then had me sitting in the driver's seat of this bucket heading north on interstate 75 toward Indy.

I was excited to be hitting the road. I convinced Jennifer this was a great idea, and she took the bait, along with Lucy and Patrick, my partners at ai3, and Clayt, our close friend from college who shared my excitement for racing. Our introduction to RVing had begun.

After we pulled into the B camping lot south of the Indianapolis Motor Speedway to find our spot for the next three days, I was walking through the lot and came across an iconic little trailer that just seemed to have it going on. The retro styling was cool, with teardrop lights, chrome trim, and exposed riveted aluminum skin, and the air about the shiny potato expressed a confidence that was unique. I'm not exactly sure it was confidence, but it was its own thing. It stood alone in a field of bland RV campers with poorly designed paint jobs designed to distract the eye from the fiberglass box it really is. This silver trailer was simply cool as hell, and I was hooked.

I researched the trailer after we arrived back in Atlanta, scouring through Websites and forums to find out more on what I now knew was a 16-foot Bambi Airstream. I appreciated the design, but it was the pure utility that turned me on, and the daydreams began shortly after. For the next year I didn't pursue the idea of buying an Airstream much, given that my plate was full with working on my own business, and I thought that finding large blocks of time to drive around the country just wasn't in the cards.

In 2006 I was again driving a rental sleeping bucket into Lot B at the Indianapolis Motor Speedway for the USGP. This time the ladies took a rain check on the trip, and it was Patrick, Clayt, and another close friend from college, Jeff, who joined me in our Lot B RV mobile suite. As we made our way through the grass field I noticed the Airstream that started my fascination was again there, parked among the many fiberglass buckets, or Some Other Brand, as Airstreamers call them.

After our trip, I made my way back to Atlanta with a big idea in mind, one with an Airstream in the middle of it. I was determined to see the United States again from the road. I needed to scratch the wanderlust itch that was again right at the surface. I had the romantic picture in my mind of driving through the fields of the Midwest, headed toward the Rocky Mountains with a trailer in tow, eventually making my way to Yellowstone. I know this is not a unique dream in the United States—a desire to pack up and explore—and it is not a unique human feeling to want to roam and discover the world around us, which is why it was so important for me to do. I saw it as an opportunity to be reconnected to the basic essence of who we are as people and as Americans. Nonetheless, it was not the ultimate destination on my dream journey that excited me, but the unknown and unplanned experiences that would ultimately happen along the way.

I presented this master plan to Jennifer to get her excited about seeing the country and being together a little more without the distractions everyday life creates. It was not only a way for me to reconnect with a basic need I felt was important, but it was also an opportunity for us to reconnect as a couple. She politely entertained my hand-waving description of great adventures, but I think she was recounting the "Go RVing" adventure up to Indianapolis the year before, and was not interested in the least about spending any more time inside an RV, let alone a trailer. I left my ace in the hole until the end, when I walked her through the Airstream Website, pulling up sexy (yes, I said *sexy* in regard to a trailer manufacturer Website) images of the interior of the Airstream I wanted for our travels.

It helped that Christopher Deam, a talented California-based architect, had recently redesigned the interior of some of Airstream's trailers, giving them a much-needed modern aesthetic that appealed to our personal taste. Jennifer made a quick connection with the images and felt they actually looked like our own house; she was hooked as well. I moved quickly and decided to take her down to the closest Airstream dealer, located in Jackson, Georgia, about an hour drive from our loft.

Shortly after I hooked Jennifer on the idea of an Airstream, she woke up one morning with the idea of traveling around in that Airstream to write a book she had been thinking about. At the time, I was not interested in turning my idea of "reconnecting" via an adventure of thousands of miles crossing the country with an Airstream in tow into a career project. I was not mentally available to what it could be at the time Jennifer came to me with the idea.

I felt that the project that is now Carve Your Own Road was not going to give us the opportunity to truly appreciate our own freedom, but it would quickly become "work," and I was already up to my eyeballs with work, and needed an avenue to explore both the country and what I truly wanted my life to look like. Jennifer worked on me for a couple of weeks—not that she ever needed my approval, but we both knew it was a pretty big idea, and the only way it could happen was if we were in it together. I knew it was a great idea, but I was exhausted, and was digging deep to stay with building my company and personal relationships with my partners. I wasn't up for it mentally or physically, but with the intensity with which she saw the project evolve in her mind, the details were clear to her, and she was not about to let me say no.

The concept of Carve Your Own Road was pretty clear for us both, but we knew that in order to have credibility with those people and organizations we wanted to reach out to, we needed to have a big domino fall first: our partner had to be Airstream. Without their involvement, we knew we would be working uphill.

Jennifer wasted little time in finding the players at Airstream's headquarters in Jackson Center, the rural Ohio home of Airstream since 1952. Tim Garner was a huge advocate and loved our concept from the beginning, and felt that Airstream needed this type of grassroots effort to expand its brand, especially with the 30-something young professional demographic. Tim saw Airstream in a broad context, with expansion beyond camping and having a unique guest house; he saw the brand making inroads with professional organizations, and hospitality and entertainment companies that could benefit from having a mobile facility.

After several discussions with Tim, he invited us to come to Jackson Center, Ohio, for a meeting with the CEO at Airstream's headquarters. Soon, we received news that they were going to sponsor us. We were so excited and grateful for the opportunity!

Taking Delivery

We arranged to pick up our new Carve Your Own Road Airstream in Jackson Center just a few days before the 2007 United States Grand Prix. I had to work in some personal time with business—after all, if I am going to be just a few hours from Indianapolis, and it *happened* to be around the same time as a Formula One race, well, what's the harm in that? We arrived in Jackson Center a little behind schedule, which didn't sit well with Airstream's service manager. After all, he was in charge of getting us up and running with a new tow hitch and making sure everything was in good working order before we headed out.

Nevertheless, Jennifer and I were both giddy about the situation, excited to be there, but also in disbelief that we had made it this far into our project. We knew we were standing at the doorstep; picking up our Airstream meant it was time to step through the threshold and start to deliver on our plans.

After our triumphant arrival in Jackson Center, we spent an anti-climactic two and a half hours at the Airstream visitor center adjacent to the service shop checking e-mails and "inventorying" the retail center for possible future purchases, waiting for the work to be completed on our SUV in preparation for towing the trailer. I took the down time as an opportunity to brief Jennifer on her "game face" for when they pulled the Armada and Airstream out of the service bay together. It was going to be the first time we saw the full extent of what we were about to be driving around the country for the next six months, and I wanted to avoid having a "holy shit" moment in front of the people that just entrusted us with a $70,000 travel trailer. Neither of us had much experience towing anything, let alone 6,000-pound 28-foot-long trailer, but that was what this project was all about for both of us—doing things we'd never done before.

Driving away from Jackson Center, we recounted the last few months and the path that got us to where we were. We knew we could've easily sat at home and not tried to work with Airstream. We could have listened to the people around us who said, "You can't do that," or "Why is Airstream going to listen to you?" but we would've missed out on the chance to see Jackson Center, to get to know a truly iconic company, and The Table 39 Accord would have been just another dinner. We drove 55 miles per hour all the way to Indianapolis that evening, laughing. We finally had our "holy shit" moment!

A month later, we held a launch party for Carve Your Own Road and made our first round of interviews with Daryn Kagan, Phillip Chen, and Allison O'Kelly at Piedmont Park in Midtown Atlanta. We secured a shady spot near the main event fields, with a fantastic view of the Midtown skyline to the west. It was our chance to show all our friends and family that Carve Your Own Road was the real thing, a big idea that was coming to life through simple hard work, collaboration, clarity of thought, and a passion for pushing beyond what we all think is the norm. Everyone resonated with the concept; they all loved the Airstream, and they were curious and wanted to learn more: "Why Airstream?" "Where are you headed first?" "Who are you interviewing?" It was great to talk about big ideas that day. It was the first time in a long while that I was not talking shop; instead, the discussions were about people's potential, their dreams, and the opportunities we all seek to make them come to life.

It was a great afternoon. I knew we were on to something big. Of course, dreaming about doing something big is not a new concept, but we realized that having the Airstream in the park that day was the symbol of our dream, our big idea. We had our Shiny Thing in place, and it was time to take it on the road for our first trip.

Chapter 5

Biting off More Than We Could Chew: The East Coast Tour

Do not go where the path may lead; go instead where there is no path and leave a trail.

—Ralph Waldo Emerson

In Joe's Words

Shortly after the launch party, we set the schedule for our first interview road trip, a 10-day swing up and down the East Coast from Atlanta to New York. As are most novice adventurers, we had booked every day full of driving and interviews, with very little down time. We were excited about getting started, and didn't plan on how important it was to have those unplanned moments for a little exploration along the way.

Carve Your Own Road: East Coast rolled out of Atlanta with the Airstream packed full of gear for the next 10 days on a course towards Raleigh, North Carolina. We planned to spend a couple of nights there with my sister Candice and her fiancé, Nat, along with my dad and his wife, Cindi, who were visiting. We used our time in

Raleigh for some last-minute preparations, including the attachment of our official maritime flags that spelled out "Carve Your Own Road" on the curb side of the Airstream; we were officially a land barge headed north.

Jennifer and I both shared driving duty, maneuvering our way from Raleigh toward Washington, D.C.—that is, until the "incident." I am a control freak about driving; that is a well-known fact among anyone who has ever spent more than five minutes with me in a car. Just a few hours up the road, ee came to a unanimous decision (if you can call two people making a decision unanimous) that I would be the full-time wheelman for Carve Your Own Road: East Coast thanks to a small gas station in southern Virginia. Jennifer was pulling in for our first gas stop for the day (we usually had two or three for a full day of driving), when she turned in as she normally does—without a 28-foot trailer hitched on. In Jennifer's defense, nothing really happened; it was just the possibility of mowing down a couple of gas pumps with a travel trailer that triggered our discussion and subsequent decision. If you have towed anything, you know what I am talking about. If you are married, have ever been married, or been in a relationship while on a road trip, you definitely know what I am talking about. It was good to get our first incident out of the way; little did we know what was ahead of us in New York.

We arrived in Washington, D.C., on Sunday afternoon; the next day we had two scheduled interviews, the first with Ada Polla, president of Alchimie Forever, a skin-care products company, and the second with Warren Brown, author, TV host, restaurateur, and owner of Cake Love. Right after our interviews we planned to be back on the road headed to New Jersey, so we arranged to camp just north of D.C. in Maryland, about a mile from the College Park metro station. It would be easy to jump on the metro into town and not worry about driving during rush hour.

It turned out that we were not the only ones with the need to camp conveniently just outside the district. It was our first time staying at a campground near an urban center, especially one that attracts such a huge number of tourists. It was tight; not exactly a place that you would want to stay for any length of time. Nonetheless, it would do for the next 18 hours.

With the Airstream parked in Washington, we took the evening to enjoy dinner in Annapolis, Maryland, just east of D.C. on the Chesapeake Bay. I remember visiting Annapolis as a kid when my family lived in northern Virginia, so this was a bit of a homecoming for me. Annapolis has an air of confidence about it; a small, well-kept capital city that is highly regarded in history and modern culture. It is the home of the U.S. Naval Academy, where David Robinson taught many about the box and Jack Ryan taught history—well, you get the point.

Crab cakes were a requirement for dinner, and like all good *touristas* we made a line straight to an overly themed waterfront restaurant and placed a couple of orders. I am 99 percent sure we could have found a better crab cake in town, probably a block off the water, but it wasn't all about the food. We were looking for a nice atmosphere, and the place where we ended up was honestly no better than a Chili's decorated with fish nets. Okay, so it was all about the view, and there *was* a view. Mission accomplished! Later, full from mediocre crab cakes, we strolled through the docks, watching the sailboats in the harbor head home in the early evening twilight. That night we enjoyed one of the most spectacular sunsets I have ever seen. The entire sky was an intense purplish-red with the silhouette of St Anne's steeple and the Capitol dome creating an incredible backdrop to the marina. Not a bad way to kick off our week.

Monday, July 23, Washington, D.C.

9:30   Ada Polla—Alchimie Forever

11:00   Warren Brown—Cake Love

Just before 8 o'clock Monday morning we stepped out of the Airstream, loaded down with a laptop, tripod bag, and camera case, ready for our commute into D.C. to meet Ada and Warren. Jennifer looked great—we may camping in an Airstream outside of town, but she wouldn't be caught dead not looking good for an interview. That is what I love about her; she's always put together.

The Foggy Bottom metro station was full of commuters bustling along in an orderly fashion. It was very D.C.: under control and oddly quiet for a transit station. It was a nice change from MARTA (the mass transit system in Atlanta), where you typically have, at a minimum, one person who feels obligated to entertain the rest of the rail-going community through some deranged act. The sun was cracking through the buildings along 23rd Street and starting to heat up the city. As sweat started to bead on my head, I had flashbacks of summers in D.C. being miserably hot and humid.

We arrived at Ada's office about 9:15, giving us a few minutes to cool off from the walk and set up our equipment. The plan for our interviews was for Jennifer to ask the questions while I tried to record the answers on film. Simple enough, except I had never filmed anything before, let alone recorded sound through microphones, but that was the deal, so I figured it out.

Ada was a great interview; she was honest and authentic, which made Jennifer comfortable, giving her the opportunity to have a conversation instead of a Q-and-A, which is always pretty stiff. Ada had built a strong business in a short time, and her energy was contagious.

Warren Brown was on our schedule for 11 that morning, so we packed up the cameras, microphones, and lights, and grabbed a cab on M Street for a ride up to Cake Love, Warren's restaurant on U Street just east of Adam's Morgan. Cake Love is a funky little corner café that serves up cakes and cupcakes for those in need of a sugar high, and, judging by the traffic at 11, there is not shortage of such people. I was in need of a sugar high myself. We introduced ourselves to the manager, who was a bit perplexed as to what was going on; obviously she didn't know anything about the interview. We left a message on Warren's mobile, but got no call back. After 20 minutes we were starting to wonder if this was a no-go at Cake Love, so I ordered a cupcake to pass the time. When in Rome....

Warren flaked on his interview, despite confirming the time and place a few days before. After talking to the manager we got the impression that this isn't exactly a rare occurrence, so we left the café with the strange feeling of being disappointed and also on a sugar high. We walked down U Street to the closest metro stop and headed back to the Airstream; New Jersey was waiting.

We pried the Airstream out of our camp spot just after noon with a charted course (remember, we are in a land barge) across the Chesapeake Bay Bridge toward Smyrna, Delaware, about 40 miles northeast of Annapolis. Our goal was to reach the Jersey shore by dinnertime. We had arranged for a campsite just south of Toms River, where we would stay for the night.

Jennifer had a conference call set up with a client that afternoon, so we took this "commitment" as an opportunity to stop just on the east side of the bay bridge for an afternoon snack. We pulled the Airstream into the gravel parking lot opposite The Fisherman's Crab Deck in Kent Narrows and managed to find a waterfront picnic table that was perfect for conducting business. After a pound of peel-and-eat shrimp and a conference call, we were back on the road headed toward Delaware. I was not up to speed on Delaware—who from the South is?—besides the fact that the infamous "monster mile" is in Dover. The travel author Bill Bryson put it perfectly in *The Lost Continent*: "As I drove across Delaware now I could feel it vanishing from my memory as I went." Being the head of tourism in Delaware could be a part-time job. Anyway, it stood proudly between New Jersey and us, so we made a pass through. Lucky for us, we discovered Delaware was a hotbed of new free-standing Starbucks locations that could provide a well-caffeinated rest stop to check e-mails and make a couple calls.

It was early evening when we arrived at our campground in Toms River. Plenty of time to cook a nice dinner and whip up a small campfire. It was actually chilly on the shore, a nice contrast to the heat earlier in D.C. After dinner we pulled out a couple of blankets and lounged outside in our camp chairs by the fire. It wasn't long before we were both asleep.

Tuesday, July 24, Red Bank, N.J.

1:00   **Marcia Blackwell—Blackwell's Organic**

3:00   **John Willig—Literary Services, Inc.**

Our third interview was in Red Bank, New Jersey, at Sickles Market, with Marcia Blackwell from Blackwell's Organic. We drove the 40 miles from Toms River up to Red Bank on Tuesday morning for a 1 o'clock interview. We arrived to an amazing welcome. Sickles Market and Marcia had really pumped up our arrival with everyone at the market. We were "road royalty," and it felt great after the last few days of driving! We maneuvered the Airstream into a series of coned-off parking spaces adjacent to the market's original farmhouse. We pulled the awning out and set up our table and chairs facing a well-groomed lawn lined with perennials and pine trees. Our hosts at Sickles brought lunch and enough snacks and sweets to last us the next 10 days! It was a wonderful discussion, and we learned a lot from Marcia about manufacturing organic foods—in her case, gelato and sorbetto—and the passion she has for her business.

Later that afternoon, John Willig, our literary agent, picked us up for a tour of the Jersey shore from Monmouth Beach south to Avon-by-the-Sea. John gave us the history of Asbury Park, driving by the boarded-up buildings where Bruce Springsteen played in his earlier years and inspired his first album *Greetings From Asbury Park*. We walked through the historical streets of Ocean Grove, past the shops and summer hotels on Main Street to the Great Auditorium, the central building of a Methodist oceanfront summer camp that was originally founded in the late 1800s. The camp was made of unique tent cabins that are no bigger than our Airstream, decorated with striped awnings of bright primary colors, and the majority of them had a fresh American flag blowing in the ocean breeze off the front porch. It was a uniquely American scene that I had thought was long gone.

We ate dinner with John at a place with a nice view of the ocean that evening. Our discussion centered on our plans for the book and also our strategy for entering into New York City that night.

Our plan was to let traffic die down enough to drive into the city from Red Bank with as little stress as possible. We figured that leaving around 9 o'clock would have us entering the city around 10:30 or 11 p.m., perfect timing to get parked and get a decent night's sleep before our busy two days of interviews. Oh, the naiveté—this was NYC after all!

Before we left Atlanta, Jennifer had consulted with an Airstream dealer in New Jersey about the best strategy for driving to Manhattan with a trailer. Keep in mind, we had two large propane tanks sitting on the frame between our SUV and the trailer. Highly flammable tanks are not exactly on the New York Port Authority's top 10 things to let through a tunnel, especially in the post 9/11 world we live in. But we were assured it could be done, you just need a little advice from an insider who has done this kind of thing before: "You should have no problem with the Holland Tunnel, just go through late at night when the traffic is light" is the advice we received. We headed up the Garden State Parkway from Red Bank at about 9:30 that night. To my surprise, I was nervous about this part of the trip. I'm usually excited about the prospect of driving in the chaos of a major city and finding my way on unfamiliar streets, but this was my first time with a trailer in tow, and we still had to get the trailer parked, which isn't exactly a quickie job.

Pier 61, the large sports and events complex situated along the Hudson River in Chelsea, was to be our home base while we were in the city. It was a great spot, with easy access to Soho and Midtown, and the location didn't require us to maneuver the "Carve Your Own Road Land Barge" through the streets of Manhattan; all we had do was cross the Hudson via the Holland Tunnel and make our way north on West Street for 20 blocks—piece of cake, especially late at night.

Making our way off the New Jersey Turnpike at exit 14C, we squeezed our way into the tollbooth (which seemed to have all of an inch clearance on each side of the trailer) to drop our $8.20 bail to set us free for the drive along the Pulaski Skyway to the entrance to the Holland Tunnel.

The view of lower Manhattan was simply amazing from the skyway; it was a clear enough night that you could see the lights of the Verrazano Narrows Bridge crossing from Staten Island to Brooklyn in the distance; the spire of the Chrysler Building was shining bright, along with the towers in Midtown around Times Square, but it was the Empire State Building sitting straight in front of us that captured my gaze. Jennifer and I were both excited to finally be here. We skipped ahead on the iPod to Ryan Adams's song *New York, New York* from his album *Gold* (sorry, Frank) to complete the scene. We had arrived. Kind of.

As we approached the Holland Tunnel, the lanes through the tollbooths seemed to be tighter than at the turnpike, but I managed to center the Airstream and slide up to the pay booth. I handed over our toll, and as the attendant took a second look, she asked, "What is under that cover in front of the trailer? That's not a propane tank is it?" Crap! So here is a moment we all face from time to time: I felt the BS on the tip of my tongue, ready to dish a few lines to talk our way through. As I readied my story, I took a quick glance out of the windshield and saw a Port Authority police officer stepping out of his car and walking towards us. We had done nothing wrong, but the anxiety was a little high. If we don't get through here what was plan B?

Before I could respond, the attendant handed back our money as she instructed us to see the officer at the inspection lane just off to the side of the toll plaza. The officer simply instructed us about the ban on propane tanks in the tunnel and told us we needed to find another way onto the island. We gave him our little story about how this was the route recommended to us by a local dealer, yadda yadda yadda...he "recommended" we try the Lincoln Tunnel and waved us on our way—that is, on our way to the turnaround lane for our trip back to the turnpike.

Finding our way north on the turnpike after our third tollbooth squeeze of the evening, a quick time check showed it was about 11:15. I was wiped out from our day, we had been at this for the better part of 15 hours since leaving Toms River, and I knew we were running out of steam. Our excitement was wearing off, and I felt the anxiety rising quickly.

Toll booth squeeze number four took place at NJTP exit 17, about 13 miles further up the Hudson. We handed over $7.20 to see if the Lincoln Tunnel was going to be a little nicer to us than the Holland. Checking the navigation, we knew that if we could take the Lincoln Tunnel it would place us on the island in Hell's Kitchen just north of Pier 61—no problem. But not so fast...after meeting our second Port Authority officer of the night at the Lincoln Tunnel, Jennifer decided to weigh in on the situation and give her assessment of the propane and trailer restriction to the officer through my window, while she was sitting in the passenger seat. Knowing we were in need of a plan C, I was already trying to decide on the next steps, so I only caught a few parts of what she was saying, and was thankful that the officer didn't catch any of it.

We will now refer to this as "incident 2." To his credit, the officer gave us clear direction to head north to the George Washington Bridge and assisted us in making our second tunnel u-turn of the night. But unlike the Holland, the Lincoln Tunnel didn't have a turn-around lane. With arms outstretched and his traffic whistle blowing, the officer walked out on to the toll plaza in front of at least at dozen lanes of traffic trying to head into the tunnel. He shut down each lane as we slowly made a long, sweeping left turn to make our way into the westbound lanes, away from Manhattan. At one point we were literally 90 degrees to the traffic; Airstream can't *pay* for this kind of PR!

You guessed it; we squeezed through the tollbooth for the sixth time on our way back on to the turnpike heading north—so I had thought. In my state of frustration I took the ramp headed south back toward Newark and away from the George Washington Bridge. We made our way off the turnpike, dropped another $2.50 at the seventh toll booth squeeze of the night, and started scouting for a place to make a u-turn. The neighborhood we found ourselves in was sketchy at best. We whipped into a parking lot next to a used car dealership and managed to get headed back onto the turnpike.

Shortly before midnight, working plan C was in action. Cruising up the turnpike we looked over the navigation in the Armada to find out exactly where the bridge was going to drop us into the city. The GW Bridge crosses from New Jersey into Harlem at 179th Street about 7 miles north of Pier 61. Provided we could easily get onto the Henry Hudson Parkway headed south without too much trouble, we were golden. As the only non-tractor-trailer heading onto the bridge, we knew we would have no trouble crossing. After two and half hours of trying and re-trying, we finally drove onto Manhattan. It had been a crazy night! We made our way south into Chelsea, laughing at ourselves for being so frustrated, and recalling Jennifer's sad attempt at negotiation with the Port Authority. It was about 1 o'clock in the morning when we backed the Airstream into its home for the next couple days at Pier 61, and I was craving a bagel!

We had to stay in a hotel in NYC instead of the Airstream, because Chelsea Piers didn't have the power we needed to run the air conditioner—it was July after all!

Wednesday, July 25, New York, N.Y.

9:30	**Gigi Chang—Plum Organics**
11:30	**Carolyn Kepcher/Jen Marr—Carolyn & Co.**
2:00	**Robin Wilson—Robin Wilson Home**

I hit the ground running the next morning, knowing that if I wasn't halfway through a coffee by 8 a.m., things would get ugly quick, so I walked from the hotel over to Harold Square for a couple of coffees and a scone. The sunlight seemed to slap me across the face each time it beamed through the buildings along 6th Avenue, but I efficiently weaved my way through people headed to somewhere as fast as possible, keeping my mission in mind. The city's change in character from when we arrived seven hours before, bright and full of energy, was surreal. When you hit the street, you can't help but get wrapped up in its energy; it's a contagious feeling.

Jennifer and I pulled our equipment off the freight elevator at the fourth floor of 52 Walker Street in Soho where Gigi had her office carved out opposite Richardson Sadeki, a well-regarded interior design firm in the city. We arrived a few minutes early and waited for Gigi. After 10 minutes we started to have Warren Brown flashbacks. Nonetheless, Gigi made it for the interview and we spent about 45 minutes together before we headed back up to Pier 61 to drop our gear before a last-minute lunch meeting we had scheduled.

Daryn Kagan had introduced Jennifer to Carolyn Kepcher the week before, because she knew we were headed to New York. Carolyn, who had become a household name after her stint on NBC's *The Apprentice,* was launching a new project, and Daryn thought we should all meet because we shared some commonalities. We grabbed lunch with Carolyn and her partner, Jen Marr, and heard about the company they were putting together to help women balance their careers and families. We had a great discussion and truly enjoyed meeting them both. Carolyn was much nicer than she appeared on television when she was on *The Apprentice.* It definitely makes you think about all the editing they do!

After lunch, we needed to find power for the Airstream, and fast. When we arrived back at Pier 61, we discovered that the power connection we had been supplied wasn't going to handle our needs. Robin Wilson was headed to Pier 61 for her interview, and it had to be at least 85 degrees in the Airstream without the air conditioning on. The maintenance guys couldn't do much to help us out, so we turned to our neighbors: the teamsters on the *Law and Order* set who happened to be preparing for the next season on a sound stage next to our parking spot.

Most of the people on the set thought we were setting up the Airstream for a celebrity's guest appearance on the show, so there was a lot of interest in the trailer. I shared our power issue with one of the crew whom I had met earlier in the day, and he told me to go into the soundstage and ask for the teamsters' boss to see if they could help out. I had zero experience with the teamsters, and my frame of reference is basically the story of Jimmy Hoffa and the mob, so I was a little hesitant to stroll onto a TV sound stage and ask for "The Boss."

Despite my hesitation, I swung open the stage door and found the first person I could to direct me to the teamsters' office. I walked into the office, which was located just off the loading dock, and explained our situation. It wasn't more than five minutes before we had four guys working on the power. The guys couldn't have been nicer, and did what they could to get us up and running. Meanwhile, Robin Wilson had arrived for her interview with us and was patiently waiting for the work to get done, so we could have a conversation without sweating in the July heat! She couldn't have been more gracious about the situation, and we thoroughly enjoyed meeting her.

Thursday, July 26

12:00   Eric Yaverbaum—Ericho Communications

The interview with Eric was energizing. He had a great story about how his family situation had played a big role in his opening his own PR firm in his backyard after years of running a big firm in the city.

After our interview with Eric we planned to head back toward Pier 61 to loiter at a Starbucks on 9th Avenue that we spied the day before to catch up on e-mail and sip on a couple of iced coffees. We had completed our interview schedule for this trip, and our goal was to use the next four days to relax a little and take our time getting home—but not before a little celebratory dinner. That evening we found a neighborhood Italian restaurant a few blocks away from the pier for a glass of Chianti and a little capellini with Bolognese. Not exactly road food, but you can't leave New York without a good Italian meal in you.

We left New York much more quickly than we had arrived; being veterans of towing an Airstream onto Manhattan, we knew exactly how to get *off* Manhattan. After packing up and saying goodbye to the crew at Pier 61, we made our way back to Harlem and onto the GW Bridge headed to our stop for the night, a campground about 60 miles outside of the city near Newburgh, New York. The Airstream, Jennifer, and I had made it through our time in Manhattan in one piece. After all the excitement and running around in the past five days, Jennifer and I were looking forward to a quiet return trip to Atlanta.

We planned to just have an overnight stay in Newburgh, do a few hours of work in the morning, and hit the road south through Pennsylvania. Given that we were sitting in a fairly dense forest and the wireless network at our campground was about as weak as an Olsen twin, we had to grab our laptops and head to the "adult's lounge" next to the campground offices to connect with the Internet. At the time, the lounge was playing host to four kids watching cartoons on a TV that should have been recycled at least 15 years ago, and a retired couple trying to figure out how to connect to the Internet with their laptop. I am not sure who was louder, but the adult lounge wasn't exactly a Zen garden of productivity. After 30 minutes we cut our losses and headed back to the Airstream to ready for the drive.

We were headed back to Atlanta the long way through eastern Pennsylvania into Maryland and down the Appalachian Mountains through Roanoke. Considering the alternative was hammering back down Interstate 95, this wasn't much of a choice. Jennifer had not traveled through this part of the country, so it was an opportunity to take advantage of the Airstream and see something new for the next few days.

We stocked up for the drive home at a fantastic farmer's market called Adam's in Newburgh. Before leaving Atlanta we had made a pact that we were not going to eat any kind of fast food on the trip. Not that we are used to hitting the drive-thru at KFC for dinner in Atlanta, but we knew that fast food was the easy way out, and often the only choice when you're on the road, and we wanted to avoid doing things that way. It's easier to pack fresh foods when you are towing a trailer with a refrigerator and some cabinet space, so we would stop for lunches at state parks or rest stops along the way and cook our meals. It was nice not to worry about finding a good meal, particularly when you're in the middle of nowhere.

The stress of juggling the interviews, driving the last six out of seven days, and trying to respond to e-mail and phone calls seemed to disappear as we traveled south down Interstate 84 through Pennsylvania. It was a Friday afternoon and we were looking forward to having a few quiet days before reaching Atlanta on Monday.

I convinced Jennifer that we should stay in rural western Maryland near Harper's Ferry for a couple of nights. It is a beautiful area along the Potomac River, but what I failed to disclose is that we were actually camping in West Virginia along the edge of the national park. Not that there is anything wrong with West Virginia, but just about everyone who is not from West Virginia knows that this state has a bit of a PR problem. I'll leave it at that for now.

The exit strategy for our trip was a night at Highland Haven, an Airstream-only campground situated in the mountains above Roanoke, Virginia. We made sure that the last night of the trip would be at a nice place. (This was a lesson learned in 2000 on a trip to Italy when we failed to secure a decent place to stay in Milan prior to flying out of Malpensa back to the States. We ended up staying at a hotel that seemed more suited for hourly rates.) Highland Haven was a perfect place for the last night on the road, and we easily brought the average age down a couple of decades.

When we arrived back in Atlanta we had covered 2,000 miles, conducted eight interviews, and driven seven out of the 10 days we were gone. The rewards were great: Jennifer and I learned about each other as we worked on accomplishing something together, considering neither of us had done such things as filming interviews or towing a trailer before. The people we met all had amazing stories that were truly inspiring and thought-provoking. We will always have a bond with the people we interviewed, and credit them for not only making their own dreams happen, but also supporting ours.

Chapter 6

The Right Balance: More Fun and Less Work on the Midwest Tour

Travel and change of place impart new vigor to the mind.

—Seneca

In Joe's Words

Back for more: this time we were tackling the heartland. We left Atlanta, headed to Minneapolis and Chicago. Jennifer secured an interview in Minneapolis with the founders of an internal company at Best Buy called Culture Rx, as well as two interviews in Chicago: one with three partners who launched a retail company called Raceline Motorworks, and one with a good friend of ours who had recently launched a finance consulting business.

The road trip mix had been changed from our East Coast trip, the biggest change being that we brought, Eifis, our 12-year-old dog, along for the ride. We also reduced our interview schedule dramatically, making time for handling work-related issues from Atlanta as well as for having some more personal time along the way. The Midwest swing was an opportunity for me to see a couple of architectural sites, which I probably would not be near again anytime soon. The first was New Harmony, Indiana, famous among architects for Richard Meier's Antheneum and the roofless church designed by Phillip Johnson.

New Harmony was a great first-night stop. It's a little more than an eight-hour drive from Atlanta and sits just at the southwestern tip of Indiana on the Wabash River. We almost had the entire Harmonie State Park to ourselves that night; I guess it pays to camp out on a weeknight, but I couldn't imagine the place ever being full.

The next morning we drove into town and stole some time to walk through the roofless church and around the Antheneum. Jennifer and I have traveled through Europe and a lot of the United States, but there was something intensely special about this place. The roofless church was a surreal experience. The silence that exists within its courtyard and the simplicity of the solution was amazing.

Johnson designed the structure in 1979, and I honestly only heard about it because it was a side note in architectural articles about Meier's visitor center. It was interesting to see a design that was about creating a "place" next to a design that was about creating an "object." Johnson's concept for the church was that "only one roof, the sky, could embrace all worshipping humanity." Johnson's concept made me question the importance of each approach to designing a piece of architecture. I was inspired by the idea that architecture in its purest sense is about creating place, a spatial experience. As can many, I can become too enamored with creating objects and forget the largest ideas; "embrace all worshipping humanity" can be expressed in the simplest of gestures. Johnson's design allowed us to create our own objects, draw our own conclusions, through silence and reflection. Is that design? I would argue that it is. As our world becomes more dense and hectic, it may be the most important type of design we have.

We crossed over the Wabash River into Illinois midmorning and readied ourselves for what was going to be a long day of driving all the way through Illinois and eventually to La Crosse, Wisconsin, about 560 miles north. In hindsight, we had no business trying to do a 14-hour drive, but we did it anyway.

About six hours into the drive to La Crosse we passed through the Mendota wind farm near Paw Paw, Illinois. I was in need of a break so it was a good excuse to pull over. We drove down a dirt farm-access road into the middle of the cornfield that surrounded the turbines. I'd never been that close to one to experience the dynamic between the green fields below and the 200-foot-tall windmill; it was a pretty amazing thing to see. It was great to understand firsthand the impact, or lack thereof, the windmills had on the landscape, as well as appreciate what it would take to produce enough power for a major city using wind: we have a long way to go!

The Wisconsin state line couldn't escape our attention, because a 30-foot-tall mouse dressed in boots and a cowboy hat holding a sign that said "Welcome to Wisconsin" let us know we had arrived. Thank God, because I would not have known by the signs that said "Cheese" at every exit along the interstate.

I am still having a mental debate about what is more bizarre to sell at a gas station, cheese or boiled peanuts (the state of Georgia is all about the boiled peanuts). All I know is that I am not interested in having a road trip longer than an hour with anyone from Wisconsin! The cheese signs started to vanish the further north we got, and the true Wisconsin was slowly emerging. The countryside was an amazing deep green, and the trees were dense and lush; it was an oasis from the farmland of Illinois we had spent the last nine hours driving through.

About 14 hours after leaving New Harmony, Indiana, we parked the Airstream at our camping spot in La Crosse, Wisconsin. It was just before midnight, and I was done. It had been a long day for all of us, and we had just beaten the weather to La Crosse; it looked as though it was going to be a long night as well.

Shortly after arriving, thunderstorms started to roll in from the west. This area of Minnesota and Wisconsin had already spent the two weeks before we arrived fighting floodwaters from the Mississippi River, and we were about to see why. We had spent a rough night in the Airstream before, but it is a trailer, and everyone knows that trailers tend to fly when things get ugly.

We lived through the storms that night despite Eifis standing at attention in the middle of our bed for most of it. Finally he sun broke through the clearing clouds, and helped liven our spirits about hitting the road again. La Crosse is only 150 miles south of Minneapolis, so we took the scenic route along the Mississippi up to Red Wing.

My only exposure to the river had been in the southern states, crossing at cities such as St. Louis and Vicksburg on Interstate 20, and Jennifer and I were both amazed at the size of the river just below the headwaters. It was great to see the beginning of something so massive and powerful, a body that most of us just take as a given, a constant that is so dynamic. We were both impressed with this part of Minnesota and happy we ventured off the beaten path to see it.

But all good things come to end, as we discovered when we arrived at the campground we had booked for the next two nights in Minneapolis. The place was a dump, and surprisingly full for being so. I propose that makes our case that it is nearly impossible to find decent accommodations for an RV within 25 or 30 miles of any major city. After Washington, D.C., we thought we had seen the worst place we would stay, but we were wrong.

The curtains stayed closed in fear of seeing something a little too "country" happening outside, especially from a neighbor who appeared to be a long-lost cousin of Sasquatch. The TV onboard the Airstream got a workout as we searched for some type of entertainment between live news programs streaming direct from the state fair.

We quickly escaped our modest accommodations, hoping the Airstream and Eifis would still be there when we returned, and headed into town in search of a little more culture—in other words, a bottle of wine and some people wearing shirts. We luckily found a spot in an old warehouse district across from Loring Park downtown.

We ate well and chatted over coffee about the interview we had the next day with Jody Thompson and Cali Ressler at Best Buy. Before heading back to our trailer, our waiter gave us a few tourist tips and mentioned that the Mall of America is a must see. My opinion of malls is that they are all crap. You can call 'em Lifestyle Centers and pepper really cute chain restaurants around them, but they just don't do it for me.

After dinner we found ourselves again beating a line of thunderstorms back to the campground. For the second straight night Eifis was not about to let us sleep until the storms had passed. We managed a few hours of sleep to add to the few the nights before, but we didn't have our interview until early afternoon—plenty of time to caffeinate.

We worked at the Airstream in the morning, trying our best to deal with the campground's wireless network, but it wasn't strong enough to make a dent in our Internet needs. Fed up, we decided that we needed to pick up a wireless card for Jennifer's computer while we were in town, so now we had our Mall of America shopping excuse.

Tuesday, August 28, Minneapolis, Minn.

11:30   Cali Ressler and Jody Thompson—Culture Rx

Arriving to Best Buy's headquarters for our interview, we were screened and tagged the same as you would be at any major corporate building before making our way into the waiting lounge. What was interesting to me was that, among all the typical vendor types wearing Dockers and embroidered golf shirts, were a bunch of kids meeting up with their parents for lunch. Pretty cool. We hit the Caribou Coffee stand that served the waiting area for a last minute shot before our interview. Cali and Jody were a blast to meet. The rapport they had was like a Seinfeld scene. They both had a great sense of humor and loved to tell their story of launching Culture Rx as a rogue initiative within the company.

After an hour we tagged out of the Best Buy complex and headed to the Mall of America as recommended twice (Jody slipped one in before we left Best Buy). It was a business trip: We needed a wireless card—and we were just too curious not to go.

It was clearly the largest mall I had ever seen. From the outside it is a huge box fortified by parking garages, but inside there is a bright skylight-covered atrium, with an amusement park complete with a log ride and roller coaster. I can see the value of this mall, especially when it is below freezing outside four months out of the year: If I experienced winters such as they have, I would find this to be a nice oasis.

While we were there we visited the Sprint store to pick up a wireless card that worked wonders, which is now known as the "Mall of America Magic Stick." With the new magic stick, Jennifer was able to work online for hours in the backseat of the Armada for the second half of the trip.

Now that our mission in Minneapolis was complete, our focus was moving on to Chicago. We had two days and a night before our first interview there, so we planned to stay overnight in Wisconsin at Mirror Lake State Park, about 40 miles north of Madison, four and half hours from Minneapolis. We didn't feel the need to loiter any longer than needed at our campground in Minnesota, so we were on the road midmorning and arrived at Mirror Lake around 3 o'clock in the afternoon. It was perfect timing to set up everything and enjoy the park. Jennifer, Eifis, and I walked around the lake and explored the park, which was just about all ours, considering it was a Wednesday night.

The drive to Chicago was only four hours from Mirror Lake, so I made arrangements for us to visit Taliesin, the home and studio of Frank Lloyd Wright, the next morning before getting back on the road. Taliesin was my second architectural must-do for this trip. Every architect studies Wright; he was the first media-age star American architect and has a massive legacy of existing work within that area, including the Seth Patterson Cottage, a small cabin at Mirror Lake designed in the late 1950s.

It is a memorable place; it had a reverence to the landscape that is unmistakably Wright. The colors and material of the home and studio seemed to blend perfectly with the farmland that surrounds the complex. I was taken aback by how humble it was and how the smallest details were designed for views away from the home to the surrounding hills. It was obvious that Wright loved this part of Wisconsin, and it's easy to see why.

That afternoon we arrived back at the Airstream and set a course for Chicago to meet up with our next interview, with Tiffany and Karl Kuelthau at their home in Downer's Grove. As we banged out a rhythm across the concrete freeways of Wisconsin headed south, we double-checked our camping arrangement for the night to confirm that our late-night arrival wouldn't be an issue. As luck would have it, it was. We hadn't planned to arrive until after 10 o'clock because our plan was to have dinner in Downer's Grove before heading to the campground. These kinds of shenanigans were completely unacceptable to our campground host, and Jennifer's power of persuasion was not making any inroads.

So we were back to square one. Our options were limited because we had Eifis with us. A few minutes of searching online, thanks to our Mall of America Magic Stick, and we found a hotel between Downer's Grove and Vernon Hills, where our next interview was the following morning.

Wednesday, August 29, Chicago, Ill.
6:00   Karl and Tiffany Kuelthau

With our overnight arrangements set we were able to relax and enjoy catching up with Tiff and Karl. We ate a casual dinner, shared our stories from the East Coast trip, and joked about our camping experience in Minneapolis. It was great to capture their story. They talked about security, insurance, and financial sacrifices they were dealing with to make a better life and be around for their kids, an important part of being an entrepreneur in this country. It was a reminder of how tough it can be on people around you when you take a leap to start a new venture.

Wheeling into the Westin hotel parking lot was a nice feeling. Jennifer gushed about taking a bath and enjoying the luxury of a nice hotel room. I was definitely on the same page. We commandeered up to half a dozen parking spaces on the outer rim of the lot, grabbed a change of clothes, and headed up to our room for the night. I had never seen a dog happier then Eifis was that night. He practically pulled Jennifer through the lobby. After six days in the car or the trailer he was loving a chance to stay at a hotel. All three of us slept hard that night. The Westin even brought up a special dog pillow for Eifis, at which he turned up his nose, and proceeded to jump up on the "Heavenly Bed" with us!

Thursday, August 30, Chicago, Ill.

10:00   Dave Domm, Rocky Jones, Blake Harper— Raceline Motorworks

The next morning we made arrangements for Eifis to be groomed for a few hours while we interviewed the founders of Raceline Motorworks: Dave Domm, Rocky Jones, and Blake Harper, in their store at the Westfield Hawthorn Mall. This was my second mall visit in three days—I was slipping fast!

The three made for a great group of guys, all very individual in their styles, but sharing a common passion for the business, a retail store concept aimed at boys centered on radio-controlled cars. They saw this as an American Girl store for boys. They swapped stories of starting out, sourcing suppliers overseas, and the pitfalls of finding the right employees.

After our interview they walked us through the steps to getting a racing license and building a custom car that you could race on the track right in the store. I was hooked. We cleared out of Raceline's shop just before a few serious-looking 8-year-old boys were to take on each other *mano y mano* on the racetrack.

Eifis looked a little angry but well groomed when we picked him up after lunchtime for our journey back to Atlanta. We were finished with our interviews, but we planned to spend a few more days on the road before arriving home: a quick overnight in Indy and two days on Lake Nolan next to Mammoth Cave National Park in Kentucky. But first I had to drive the Airstream down Lakeshore Drive and see downtown Chicago—call it a victory lap for our Midwest swing!

Chapter 7

The Stories: People Who Are Carving Their Own Roads

First comes thought; then organization of that thought, into ideas and plans; then transformation of those plans into reality. The beginning, as you will observe, is in your imagination.

—Napoleon Hill

These are the stories of many of the people with whom we spoke about their journeys into clarity (some of whom we met with on the road in the Airstream), of taking action and achieving their vision—in their own words.

We interviewed many fascinating people for this book, who told us wonderful, inspirational stories about realizing they weren't doing what they wanted and decided to make big changes, and some who received a "hard stop" and were *forced* to make a change.

Each story is a reminder of how important clarity is. When you have clarity and you've made a decision, it's as if all the doors open. I'm not saying there aren't any obstacles, but so many doors open that those obstacles appear smaller and easier to overcome.

Robin Sharma,
Best-Selling Author and Leadership Guru

I flew to Toronto to interview Robin Sharma because we wouldn't be able to make it all the way to Canada in the Airstream. I've read many of his books and have heard him speak, as well as participated in one of his weekend workshops. His personal story about how he came to be doing what he's doing today really inspired me.

Robin is one of the world's most widely read authors, and his books on leadership and personal development have been published in more than 60 languages and have helped millions of people succeed. He is also the founder of Sharma Leadership International Inc., a globally respected training firm used by organizations such as Microsoft, GE, IBM, FedEx, The Harvard Business School, Nike, and Yale University.

Prior to becoming an author and leadership guru, Robin was an attorney who found himself feeling unfulfilled and empty, asking himself if this was all there was to life.

The world outside of me caused me to become a lawyer, [though] of course I made the choice to do it. Society's ideas are if you go out there and become a professional, for example, that will lead to a life of success. If you have a nice house, nice car, etc., you will find happiness. It's so much deeper than that.

There was an emptiness inside of me; everything looked wonderful on the outside and yet inside there was this dull ache in the pit of my stomach. I found myself just going through the motions. I was saying to myself, *I've got a great education, a great job, money…is this all there is? What about waking up with a feeling of passion and what about waking up with joyfulness about what I do?*

There wasn't one "aha" moment or one defining crisis for me; it was more a gradual awareness that I needed to make some changes. My father has been big on learning and reading books. So I followed his example and started reading books on inner life, personal development, and the true meaning of success. Clarity precedes mastery. I became more clear about who I wanted to be and what I wanted my life to stand for, and also, very importantly, how I wanted to be remembered.

As a lawyer I was about driving and pushing, and what began to unfold for me was much more organic and much more balanced. It wasn't just about making a lot of money and being successful in the world. It was about liking myself and knowing my values, taking care of my health and enjoying the moments. I know that sounds cheesy but it's so important.

With the changes I made I decided to write a book to share the message, [so] I self-published *The Monk Who Sold His Ferrari*. As that book started to sell, it led to corporate engagements, and an entirely new career unfolded for me. Often when you set your goals and you become very clear about what you want, life begins to lead you. It doesn't mean you don't have to work hard; you have to take action and chase your dreams. What I found for myself was I needed to set the intention and get clear about what I wanted. Clarity is very important, then taking action, making the right choices, and working really hard.

I believe behind every excuse there is a fear. So if we fight for our excuses, we get to own them for the rest of our lives. I think our passion and our desire for our mountaintop—for whatever we want—has to be bigger than all our excuses.

We all want to know what our destiny is tomorrow. But it's a process. If you spend the time thinking, journaling, asking yourself the questions, [and] talking to people about it, you get more and more clarity.

I realized that every hour I spent doing what I don't want to do is an hour taken away from what I do want to do. Every hour spent in this office is an hour that could be spent on my dream. I know it sounds cliché, but for me that was the way it worked, and the more I said, "Here's what I stand for, here's what I want, I'm going to try to be the best I can possibly be, I'm going to try to create great value for people," doors just opened up that I didn't even know existed.

Sometimes you have to jump and the net shows up, as opposed to "Let's see the net first, then I'll jump." If you want to pursue your dream or passion, start today. It's not about starting a revolution; you don't need to leave the job today. If you were to move 1 percent closer to your dream every day, after one year you're over 365 percent closer to your dream. It's all about evolution, what I call small daily acts of greatness.

My life is so different today. I'm doing what I love to do. It doesn't mean every day is perfect, it doesn't mean I don't have challenges, but I truly feel I'm in control of my destiny. I get to live life on my own terms. I know that sounds cliché, but it's true. I actually get to make a living doing what I love to do and what I'm good at.

Allison O'Kelly, Founder and CEO of Mom Corps

Allison O'Kelly always strove to be successful professionally, and she held the same standards for herself after becoming a mother. Unfortunately, in the corporate world, she was unable to find a balance between career and family. She opted to start her own practice, serving small businesses with strategic planning, accounting, and tax services.

Prior to starting her own company, Allison earned an MBA from Harvard and went to work for KPMG as a consultant and then was hired by Toys 'R' Us, where she had various roles including launching the original Babiesrus.com Website and running an $11 million Toys 'R' Us store. She had a great background to leverage in becoming an entrepreneur. As her small business started to grow she soon hired five other women, all with families, to help serve her clients.

Over time I saw many women, mothers just like me, who wanted to stay in the workforce but didn't know how to find opportunities [that] would allow them to have balance in their lives. Because of this obstacle, many mothers leave the workforce altogether. At the same time, I noticed my clients were struggling to find high-caliber employees, and they were wondering how I was finding all these great people, and the women I brought on were wondering how I was finding all this great work. That eventually led to me creating Mom Corps. Mom Corps works to help professional moms find flexible work arrangements as well as providing a resource center, workshops, and conferences.

Everything took more time than I thought it would. It's funny; sometimes I feel like it's taken forever, and other people see how far I've come in a short time. You just take steps every day and build momentum. Long-range planning doesn't necessarily make sense for entrepreneurial companies—your goals will continually change, but the key is staying focused. It's important to read books, talk to people who have done it, bring in experts...and trust yourself.

I have more flexibility in my schedule, but I do work more. It's hard to get it off my brain. I don't know that I could ever work for anyone else ever again. Overall, it was so worth it; I've enjoyed the process and the journey of getting here. I've also had my struggles and challenges, but the benefits far outweigh those challenges.

Eric Yaverbaum, CEO of Ericho Communications

For nearly 25 years, Eric Yaverbaum has been a staple in the world of public relations. His trailblazing career has seen the birth, growth, and, finally, acquisition of a highly successful NYC-based PR agency. However, in 2007, Eric traded in his high-rise office to start a virtual agency out of his home. Why? To spend more time with his wife, who continues to battle secondary progressive multiple sclerosis, and his two children. His unconventional decision has paid off in every way imaginable.

While my wife has continued her two-decade-long battle with secondary progressive multiple sclerosis, I've learned that all the financial success in the world won't buy me one of the most important things I want in life: her health. The decision to start a new virtual agency so I could be closer to home was completely influenced by this life circumstance.

Ironically, after being home for a year I realized that money will never buy back my kids' childhood, or the precious family time that we all get ever so briefly in our lives either. Instead of missing one more little league baseball game, one more piano recital, or one more Friday night dinner with my family, I get the best of both worlds professionally and personally.

Passion, purpose, and 23 successful years of management experience running mid-size public relations agencies gave me all I needed to know to build a better business model. Leaner. Better margins. Better lifestyle. Technology not only makes running a virtual agency possible, it makes it more efficient.

When I sat my kids down to get their opinion and let them know the realities of the "risk" of leaving a very comfortable and lucrative career in NYC, my son said, "Who cares? You're better than money."

My office is on my property in the corner of our backyard. I think the separate workspace made the mindset adjustment simple. I've determined to only partner with organizations that will make the world a better place or can teach me and the 11 people we have hired (who all work from home offices) more about technology and all the ways it can be used by a PR agency and for its clients.

Marcia Blackwell, Founder of Blackwell's Organic

From working in the telecom industry to becoming a gelato entrepreneur, Marcia Blackwell's career is a testament to the power of confidence, determination, and an "I can do anything" attitude. We met Marcia in Red Bank, New Jersey, at Sickles Market, a specialty grocer who carries her products. We really enjoyed this stop;

Sickles loaded us up with fantastic food for our journey! Plus we also got to taste the gelato, some of the best stuff I've ever had!

Marcia shared her journey and gave us insight into how she dove into the food industry with little more than a passion for good gelato.

My husband, Tom, and I have always been "foodies" looking for new great places to eat, international cuisines, and new recipes. Tom is lactose intolerant and had been making dairy-free gelato and sorbet at home for several years. I had been working for a local telecom startup with fabulous coworkers, making great money, and I brought my dog to work every day. We had what you might want to call the perfect life.

However, in 2005, I was laid off from what I thought was the perfect job. The New Jersey Unemployment Office as well as my family thought it would be difficult to secure a position similar to the one I had, and all suggested I think about starting a company of my own.

After a few weeks of research, Tom and I decided to pursue starting our gelato business. Neither of us had any experience in the food industry, but I had some experience helping others start and manage companies in other industries. Our ingredients for success were a home equity loan, perseverance, and our ability to learn from other experts.

The transition was easier than I thought. The hardest part was not going to a regular office every day with a slew of coworkers. In the beginning, starting a business can be a bit isolating. So, I joined the local chapter of NAWBO—the National Association of Women Business Owners. Surrounding myself with successful people and advisors helped to motivate me to grow our business.

I was unfamiliar with just about every aspect of setting up a food business, so I started looking for experts and asking questions. I got in touch with the local Small Business Development Center to set up my LLC. I also reached out to the Rutgers Food Innovation Center to establish good manufacturing practices and to help me with other hurdles along the way. I also aligned myself with other food entrepreneurs so we could share ideas and give feedback.

Today, I get calls all the time from individuals who want advice on how to take their product to market. I tell them that having a great business idea or product does not guarantee success. It takes many people to create a great product and a profitable company. Each individual in each department of a business is important, from the lowest to the highest employee. If something goes wrong or right along the chain of command, then the ripples are felt up and down the line. I have seen this in each of my careers, but most strongly in my previous job.

It is very hard for me to separate my business and personal life. I value my free time and time spent with my family. So it just makes sense that I value the time my employees share with those important to them. I make certain buying decisions, preferring organic, Fair Trade, and locally grown food for my home, and those criteria automatically transfer over to the business. I would not feel comfortable any other way.

Sometimes I get calls from salespeople who tell me they can help increase our profit margin, but when I inquire, they often want me to substitute ingredients of less quality or use flavorings rather than the real fruit. I take the time and explain it to them. But often it is hard for them to understand that it's not just about the bottom line.

I had to learn to focus on the big picture as well as the individual tasks at hand. I had to have patience and recognize the long-term results of my efforts. This is often a struggle because many of us are taught at a young age to look for results right away. The desire is high for instant gratification.

Having a successful business is like growing a garden. It needs to be nurtured and watered. Sometime plants struggle to grow in a particular area of my garden at home. I'll make note and then move them to another place where I think they will thrive. The power of observation is key.

Owning a business forced me to focus on the larger responsibility to the community, our employees and our customers. For example, I have many more people to whom I feel responsibility. We have many customers (individuals, distributors, and retailers) that expect a delicious organic frozen dessert with minimal impact on the environment, and I feel the pressure to make sure they get that.

I think our life has changed dramatically since we started Blackwell's Organic. My relationship with my spouse is actually stronger than it was before. We have learned to communicate more effectively. Many married couples never get to see their spouses at work. Tom gets to see me "in action" and I get to learn more about him and admire his qualities as well. My horizons have been broadened by the new and interesting people that have entered our lives. I learned so much more than I ever thought I would. I get more inspired every day.

Blackwell's Organic Raspberry Sorbetto was awarded the 2008 sofi Gold award for Outstanding USDA-Approved Organic Product by the National Association of the Specialty Food Trade (NASFT) at the 36th annual Summer Fancy Food Show in New York.

Daryn Kagan, CNN Anchor Turned Online Media Entrepreneur

In 2006, Daryn Kagan was at the height of her career as a successful news anchor at CNN. However, in January of that year, Daryn learned that her contract with the network would not be renewed. Shocked, Daryn asked herself, *What's the next chapter for me?* Surprisingly, she decided not to pursue another traditional news job and instead created DarynKagan.com—an online news site devoted to delivering stories and profiles on inspiring people across the globe.

When we interviewed Daryn in Atlanta, we asked her to share some thoughts about her journey from having a successful career in television news to becoming an inspiring, thought-provoking entrepreneur.

My leaving CNN was an unusual journey. First, they told me in January 2006 that they weren't going to renew my contract, which wasn't up until a year later. To my surprise, they wanted me to stay and finish it out. In all my years there, I had never seen that. Usually, with an on-air talent, once they decide you are out, a security guard escorts you out of the building that day. They might have to pay out your contract, but they don't want you on the air. CNN's asking me to stay was both an act of trust, in that they trusted me to be professional and not flip out on the air, and it was [also] a gift.

I did not waltz out of the boss's office that day saying, "Oh, I know, I'll go start an inspirational news Website!" Hardly. The months I stayed on gave me the time to figure out the next chapter. First, I figured out what I didn't want to do—go get another traditional news job. It had been an amazing run, but talking about doom and gloom all day no longer fit who I was as a person.

Then, I started getting little pieces of inspiration. And, this is the thing I really wish I understood at the time: inspiration comes in pieces, not in one package tied with a bow sitting at your front doorstep.

It can also come from the most unlikely of places. The very first idea for DarynKagan.com came from looking at a Website based on war...I kid you not. In 2006, Yahoo! had a site called "The War Zone with Kevin Sites." Kevin had been a war correspondent for CNN and NBC, among others. Yahoo! set up a site where it said, "One Man; One Year; One Idea: Go to Every Bad Place in the World." I'm paraphrasing a bit, but the basic idea was he went from war zone to war zone filing reports.

I looked at that and thought, *You can do that? Have a specialized reporting site like that? What would mine be?* My favorite stories had always been inspirational ones...I thought, *Why not "One Woman; One Year; One Idea: Go to Every Inspiring Place in the World"?* I actually talked my way into Yahoo! executive offices and tried to give my idea away. They passed. Thank goodness! That's when my #1 biz advisor, my little sister, Kallan, said to me, "What are you doing? Why are you giving this away? Do it yourself!"

I knew nothing about launching a Website, had never even owned my own company. Ultimately, this seemed the best way to go because I figured I didn't have to get picked: not picked to get hired, not picked to do a certain story. I loved that part.

People often ask, "Weren't you scared to go for your dream and not go get another traditional news job?" Actually, no. I would've been scared to stay in TV news. Here's why: (1) I would know I wasn't following my dream, and (2) I could see where the biz is going—because of cutbacks and technology, jobs like I had are going away or going to people who are younger and/or cheaper.

Honestly, I just followed my heart. I asked myself what I wanted to do and just forged ahead. I don't think I ever really did a business plan per se. But I did do a Belief Plan. I think this was key—putting my values, priorities, and intentions on paper to commit to the kind of biz I wanted to do and why I was in business in the first place. I highly recommend that exercise.

I'm most excited about the release of my first book, *What's Possible! 50 True Stories of Real People Who Dared To Dream They Could Make a Difference.* Also, my second documentary, *Solartown USA*, will air this year.

Since leaving CNN my life in some ways has changed a ton. My commute is eight seconds—upstairs to downstairs, usually in jeans and a T-shirt. I spend my days talking to and interviewing inspiring people, rather than reporting doom and gloom.

Holley Henderson, Founder of H2 EcoDesign

Holley Henderson is a young entrepreneur who stepped out of a corporate interior design role to pursue her passion for environmental design. Since then, she's founded H2 EcoDesign, a consulting firm that is a catalyst for environmentally positive change within the building industry.

Today, Holley's passion is challenging the building industry to think about its direct impact on the environment. With a successful venture behind her, she spends much of her time speaking at industry events across the globe. Holley is known for mobilizing the audience to action and inspiring a focus on sustainability in their day-to-day work.

Holley shared with us some thoughts about her journey from having a successful "career" to becoming an inspiring, thought-provoking entrepreneur who is effecting change across the globe.

The sequence of events is really interesting because you don't see it until it unfolds. I wanted to be an artist and decided I'd rather do that for pleasure versus vocation. I decided to go into interior design, but realized it wasn't my calling.

As you grow up, you get stuck, and you look at the people above you and ask yourself, "Do I really want to live the lives they live?" But the schools set you up to think that's normal. Our entire educational system doesn't support entrepreneurship; it's really focused on getting a corporate job. Now, fast-forward several years, and I'm in a nice corporate job, but it's not my life's calling.

Because my dad left [our family when I was young], it was almost like I [felt I] had something to prove. So, I focused my drive on interior design—and it wasn't even what I wanted to do! After I realized this, I read *Zen and the Art of Making a Living*. It helped me ask the right questions to figure out what career was right for me and narrow my focus into what I'm doing now: teaching, public speaking and environmental design.

What was interesting was I started with zero knowledge, zero education on this environmental thing. It was an evolutionary process for me. I realized, by doing this environmental consulting work, I will be affecting a lot of interior designers instead of just one project at a time. In the end, my time being an interior designer was an important step for me. It wasn't my true calling, but it was part of the process I had to go through to be effective in what I'm doing today. I see that now.

Crazy things like insurance seemed like big obstacles back then. In reality, these things aren't really these huge issues that you make them out to be. I think, for me, it was scary because I didn't have the family foundation or anyone to back me up financially. But the good thing was that I had no one depending on me, so it really was a good time. Worse case scenario, I could always go back to a corporate job pretty easily if I needed to. The timing aligned and my fears were allayed.

Changing my mindset about my growth as a business has also been a challenge. The work itself has not been a challenge; it has been wonderfully easy. I didn't take a loan out to do this either, so there were days when I was wondering how I was going to pay the rent. But everything has worked out beautifully.

I cashed out my 401(K), and it was just enough to get started with very little left over. I didn't have any savings. It truly was a complete leap of faith. But it all just fell into place. I did accrue a little credit card debt, and I really had to budget for things, but I didn't suffer. It wasn't a big lifestyle change for me.

I have a very big spiritual connection, and I feel like I was meant to do this. I don't really market a whole lot. I think public speaking is a natural marketing effort for me. There is something about doing what you're meant to do that makes it easy. People see your energy and enthusiasm and they help you out and you get business. Being aligned in professional organizations and being involved in the community has helped a lot too. I don't have a lot of overhead; things are tight and efficient. The combination of the project work and speaking has been the key for me; they are synergistic in my mind.

The flexibility and freedom I now have is huge. I also really feel like I'm making a difference. Being on my own instead of inside a company, I feel like I can be so much more efficient and I can control my environment so much better. I get so much more done and can take an afternoon off if I want to. I also have the ability to say no. When you work for someone else, it's much harder to do that. I can say no to things that are not in alignment with my mission.

Ada Polla, Cofounder of Alchimie Forever

Ada Polla started out doing consulting and product management in the medical device industry, when she realized that the corporate route was not for her. She is now the co-creator of the Swiss antioxidant skin care line Alchimie Forever. She developed the line's brand and visibility, and established international distribution for the products (securing flagship retailers such as Fred Segal Spa in Los Angeles, Henri Bendel in New York, and Sephora in France), and has driven the company's double-digit annual revenue growth. We caught up with her when we were in Washington, D.C., and her passion and excitement for what she's doing came through clearly.

I worked at two different corporate jobs out of college and found that I was pretty bored and that it just wasn't for me. While I was in business school I decided to make the transition to running my own company. During my first year I started taking action on that goal by doing a ton of research and writing my business plan, and then during the summer I worked on my Website and developed the product line. I started selling products and doing marketing the second year of business school. I did the work part-time while being in school to be sure it was viable. Taking action on my ideas made it clear to me that I was on the right path.

What you imagine and what you write on paper is not always what happens, but it serves as a guiding vision; the actuality of what I originally wrote has evolved. Forcing myself to write everything down was great for me; it's been an important disciplinary step. It gave me a place to go back to and look at my vision and reconnect with it.

I've also realized [that] another thing that's really important is a network of support. I started a group when I was in business school called the New Network of Entrepreneurial Women. One of my friends who was part of the group had decided she didn't want to be a lawyer anymore. She wanted to open a boutique store that sold designer samples, but she had just found out she was going to be made partner if she stayed for a while.

She was thinking it wasn't the right time and I told her it's never the right time; you can find excuses at any point in your life. If you start rationalizing and thinking about what could go wrong at any point in time, it's just not going to happen. I always tell people, go and do it! I'm happy to say she opened her boutique and she recognized how important it was to have that network of support.

Randy Hain, Managing Partner of Bell Oaks Executive Search

Randy Hain is the managing partner and an owner of a very successful executive search firm in Atlanta. Throughout the years he has earned a reputation as a values-based leader who invests heavily in his coworkers, candidates, and clients. Most search firms aren't known for their commitment to values and creating a good work environment for their employees; it's a pretty tough industry in that regard.

Randy was leading recruiting for a large national restaurant chain that had more than $900 million in revenue when he made the decision to make a change. He had one child at the time and was working long hours and traveling a huge percentage of the time. He decided to be very intentional about his approach to finding the right opportunity that was in alignment with his values. After finding what he was looking for, his life has changed for the better, and his family is flourishing as well.

For years I took the classical approach to the career ladder. For some reason I thought that everyone traveled 80 percent of the time and worked at least 70 hours per week. After my first son was born I realized I wasn't being the father my father was to me, so I decided to be very intentional about looking for a new job that served my family first. Also, one of my children is a special-needs child, and my need to be present for him is very important.

I created criteria for that new job, and I measured every opportunity against it. There were four things I was looking for:

- Work/life balance.
- Company with a values orientation.
- Company not afraid to evolve and grow.
- Uncapped income potential.

It took me over a year to find the right fit that matched my criteria, and the company I joined had everything I was looking for and lots of potential. Today, this company is the exact opposite of all of my bad job experiences, and what's really great is I've played the lead role in building the culture of this organization. We have established a great reputation for integrity, community involvement, and thought leadership in the business community. For the last two years in a row, we've been named one of the Best Places to Work in Atlanta by the *Atlanta Business Chronicle*. That makes me really proud because the employees confidentially vote and share feedback to an independent research firm on how they view the company.

I think we're different from most companies because we celebrate work/life balance and offer flexible schedules. We feel like our employees are parents/husbands/wives first and employees second, and we've set up our environment and culture to support that. We've also made community involvement a big part of our culture, and that really resonates with our employees. I've never been more fulfilled in my life. I'm living my life in alignment with the priorities I've set for myself, and I've been able to make a tremendous impact at my company and in the community. Also, I don't travel, and am at home for dinner every night—I can't tell you how good that feels.

Recently, I've unlocked a passion for writing and speaking I never knew I had. I'm allowing my creative side to flow, and it's very fulfilling. I think I've been able to connect with that part of myself because everything in my life is in alignment.

Karl Kuelthau, Financial Planner
for Northwestern Mutual

Karl Kuelthau followed the prescription for success, got a great education, and had a successful, high-paying career in investment banking and private equity. After his wife, Tiffany, became pregnant with their first child, he realized that if he stayed in his current role, he wouldn't be able to spend the kind of time he wanted to spend with his growing family. He and Tiffany sat down and took the time to create a new vision for what he wanted in his career and the lifestyle they wanted for their family, and set out to make it happen.

Tiffany and Karl live in Chicago, where we had dinner and got to spend some time with their two children, Taylor and Jack. It's easy to see how their commitment to family has paid off for the entire family.

Tiffany and I were clear that we wanted a lifestyle [such that] she could stay home with the kids. So, when she had our first child [and] she resigned from her position, it was an easy decision to make for us. My career has always been in different shades of finance, investment banking, and private equity. I was working for an investment banking private equity firm and I had gotten to the point where I didn't enjoy the lifestyle working for someone else. I didn't [like] having someone else dictate [the] hours I worked, my vacation time, etc.

When Tiffany was pregnant, the thought of a lifetime of having to ask someone else for permission when I wanted time off made me decide that it was time to make a change. I didn't want to be in the position of asking when I could take vacation, when I could leave work, or having our vacations cut short or cancelled. The industry I was in is known for long hours and missed vacations, and I didn't want that for us. I knew I could stay in the same industry and switch firms, but it still wouldn't have given me the flexibility I now have.

It took me 10 months to make the final decision to leave my job to start my own business in financial planning and wealth management; I wanted to be really sure that I was making the right decision. It was pretty scary at first. It was easy to quit on the one hand—it was easy to walk away from something I knew wasn't the best thing for my family or me. What wasn't easy to walk away from was the comfortable living we had, and putting that at risk.

Making the leap into this new venture went great from the standpoint of loving what I was doing and being successful from most of the metrics that had been set for the industry I'm now in. The financial aspect was tough though. Faith in the company and faith in the fact that we had made the right decision and in the long term things would be the way we wanted them to be, kept me moving forward every day.

Our vision for me to have time with our family as our kids grow up, being at their soccer games, taking nice vacations, and being able to live my life the way I want to, is very meaningful to Tiffany and me. I have [a] clear picture of financial freedom and having all the time I want with my family; it's very compelling, and it's great seeing that vision coming to fruition. I see progress being made every day.

I'm working harder now than I did before, but I'm very excited and much happier with what I'm doing. I'm enjoying the actual day-to-day work and working toward my goals. It's fun to develop new relationships and make your own decisions, work with the people you want to work with. You also rise and fall based on your own decisions, and I think that's a great way to live life!

Tiffany says that she loves seeing him happy with what he's doing and seeing his passion for his work. "I love when he comes home and he's so excited about what he's doing. It's been challenging also; I have two kids at home and he's out there trying to make it happen. I look to him to keep me focused on the vision and hearing how we're moving toward it. It makes me happy that he wants to do so much for our family and he's working for our future while doing something he loves to do. He's trying to do this all for all of us and I admire that."

Blake Harper, David Domm, and Rocky Jones, Cofounders of Raceline Motorworks

Founders Blake Harper, David Domm, and Rocky Jones launched Raceline Motorworks in 2005 with the goal of creating a totally personalized and interactive environment for kids. Raceline Motorworks is a new concept store that provides kids a place where they can design, build, and race their very own remote-controlled cars in a fun environment.

The store offers a full on/off-road test-drive track, plus a showroom and assembly area where children can choose their own car; select their own body; colors, decals, and tires, and then build it with the help of the staff. In addition to their own car, each child walks out of the experience as an owner—with a driver's license, title to the vehicle, and full membership to a club for kids who like to race vehicles with their friends in and outside of the Raceline Motorworks store.

We met Blake, David, and Rocky at their store in Chicago. These three guys left very good, high-paying careers to launch this business. The three of them of have complementary skill sets and all are passionate about the business.

Passion for the business is a key ingredient to Blake, who previously had a successful career in management consulting.

I had great jobs, and had been very successful in my career, but there was just something missing. Today we're building a business, and it's pretty cool because [in] this business you have dads in the store interacting with their kids. When we're at a party for one of our league nights, top of my mind is seeing a lot of kids and parents having fun. That's what drives us. Day to day, you're running a business, but at the end of the day, the reason we did this is because it had a certain vibrance to it and we're passionate about it. There's more to it than just dollars and cents.

David had a career in private equity before cofounding Raceline Motorworks, and he's happy about his choice to become an entrepreneur and to be doing something impactful.

When you start any kind of company, you're building something. At the end of the day, you're filling a need, and with this business I'm creating purpose. What we're doing is having an impact on the world in our own particular way. There are days when I'm walking back from Starbucks and heading back to the office and I get this feeling like, wow, this is our company! I get filled with this excitement and feeling like the world is my oyster. You have your critics and your bad days, but that passion and excitement pulls me through.

Rocky, who held roles in retail operations prior to joining the group, talks about how passion is a key driver for success.

It's important to start something you believe in, your hobby or your passion. If you're just doing it to do it, it's not going to work out. You won't be happy at midnight or 2 a.m. when you have to work on it. It's paramount that you get enjoyment out of it.

They created a business plan that helped them to get funding, but the direction morphed from the original plan. "You have to be open to that and making adjustments as you go; you're growing from [the] initial model," said Rocky. Blake and David agreed: "We're constantly refreshing our thoughts about the business plan and evolving it every day. It changed as part of speaking with trusted advisors and getting feedback from the market. It's a process, not a document."

Chapter 8

Inside Out: A Grassroots Approach to Major Transformation

Personal transformation can and does have global effects. As we go, so goes the world, for the world is us. The revolution that will save the world is ultimately a personal one.
—Marianne Williamson

Cali Ressler and Jody Thompson have an amazing story of transformational change, both for themselves and for their company. These two women embarked on a mission to change the world of work inside Best Buy by using an unsanctioned, grassroots approach, and they changed the culture of the company. With their success they were able to launch their own company, called Culture Rx, with the help of Best Buy. They've also coauthored a book called *Why Work Sucks and How to Fix It.*

We interviewed Jody and Cali at the Best Buy corporate headquarters in Minneapolis, Minn. After reading about their story in an article in *Time* magazine, we were very intrigued. They were both working in an HR function at Best Buy when they came together to work on a pilot program focused on work/life balance. Little did they know that their coming together would start them down a path that would transform the culture of Best Buy, launch their own consulting company, and lead them to coauthor a book.

Their vision is to create a workplace where nothing matters except great results, and their strong belief is that there is a better way to do so. People everywhere want better lives, and employers want better results; through the program Cali and Jody have created, they think neither side has to compromise.

What they've been able to accomplish is nothing short of miraculous, and is a testament to having clarity and a vision for what you want to accomplish using the power of passion to make it happen. We thoroughly enjoyed the interview with them; they were very funny and passionate about this topic, at times doing some great role-playing about what the work culture is really like. We totally related to their stories!

This all started for them when Best Buy conducted a survey asking their employees what the company could do to become the employer of choice. The highest thing on the list was "trust me to do my work and live my life the way I see fit." When the executive team read the data they thought it was interesting that their employees didn't care more about money, perks, or benefits. What they wanted was something intangible, and it was clear it would be hard to get their arms around. A year after that survey, the executives realized that trust is foundational, and it's hard to start a program around it.

Some of the leaders wanted to do a flexible work arrangement pilot with a group of employees because work/life balance was also an issue, so 320 people were launched into a pilot program that included telecommuting, flex time, a compressed work week, and a reduced work week. Everyone in the group got to select a schedule. However, there was still a strong focus on the number of hours worked and being sure it was Monday through Friday.

The six-month pilot was rocky at times; people were trying to prove they were working by sending out more e-mails, more spreadsheets, and so on. But the participants of the pilot did show higher engagement, productivity, and morale. Following the pilot, the task was to implement this idea across corporate headquarters. Cali said she knew that something needed to move forward; people's lives had changed and she felt that they had to explore it. Jody and Cali had seen firsthand the wonderful things that had happened to people's lives and the strong business results that followed.

They got together to discuss making an adaptive change plan, realized it was the right thing for everybody, and knew it had to happen. With what they wanted to do, they knew it had to be a grassroots effort. They decided to go down a path that wasn't sanctioned, and for some reason weren't worried about losing their jobs. "We didn't worry about it because all we could see was the end game of what this could really look like for people, communities, society, and so on. We did this in a very grassroots way, completely unsanctioned by upper management," Jody said.

Every once in a while there was a concern about their livelihood, because they knew they were going against the grain. "We had to hold fast and true to our belief since we knew there were a lot of people that were going to try to shut us down," Cali said. They were working to give employees more control, and management less control, and the management team had them writing a bunch of white papers and business cases in the beginning, likely as a way to slow them down.

Cali said, "We spent a lot of time going back and forth about what we saw as the end vision. We knew that anyone who opts to work nontraditionally gets a stigma attached to them. Immediately comments start erupting all over the place: 'Oh, bankers' hours again?' That language exists in cultures all over the place. We had two big ideas; people should be focused on results, and we need[ed] to tackle [that] language." They had their ears to the ground for leaders who were progressive, and several had expressed interest in putting something in place in their groups. "We didn't have weighted business cards: We were just two peons from HR who had a great idea, and they listened to us!"

"You begin with your idea and talk to people about it; that's how you create change," Jody said. "When you have a deeply held belief and are passionate about something, you can be fearless and take action. Our deeply held belief and confidence about what we wanted to do made people listen to us."

They had noticed that managers believe people should be at their desks in order to be getting their jobs done, which is a 1950s approach. Cali and Jody decided to give them a new frame to look at: the Results Only Work Environment (ROWE). In the ROWE model people are able to do what they want, when they want, as long as the work gets done—they don't have to ask permission.

"The first question that came up from the managers when introduced to this new model was, 'How do we know what people are going to be doing?' We asked them how they knew what people are doing now. They realized they didn't know, but [think that because employees are] in their cubes, they've got to be doing something; they're here and they're following the rules. The managers felt like they owned their employees' time, but what needed to shift was that they needed to be focused on what gets done. Quit worrying about monitoring the hallways, but instead monitor the work and productivity."

The managers then saw Cali and Jody as helping them to figure out how to know what their employees were doing. All the tools were already in place; there was a performance and development guide no one was using. The guide had been meaningless to the managers with the foundation so screwed up, so the managers in the program were now excited about using it. "We took the carpet out from under them, [so] they had to grab on to some of these tools," Jody said.

The company had been measuring its employees on what *looks like* work: If an employee was on time and sitting in his or her cube, he or she was working because that looked like work. Cali and Jody had to reframe for the managers what work looks like and how it's measured. "We have to change the idea that just because people showed up at the building, they're working. In the ROWE model we got rid of the time clock and focused instead on whether or not the work was getting done."

After implementing the ROWE model into certain groups, they found that when people were free to do work in any way they want to, they were becoming so efficient that they were having a hard time getting to 40 hours. The employees in the program were telling them that they were getting more done and were looking to take on more work.

Still, it was a tough road because everyone was so focused on the 40-hour work week even though people were becoming much more efficient. Jody says, "40 hours is just sort of an arbitrary number. If I'm working less, I'm a slacker. If I'm working more, I'm a producer. It could be the person that works 60 hours doesn't get a whole lot done; that's really just presenteeism, not productivity."

Jody and Cali feel strongly that it makes no sense to be tracking anything by time. They can't understand how you would mark on a timesheet a great idea you came up with that took five seconds, but could ultimately have a huge impact on the company. Jody asks, "What are we focused on? What's really important? We're focused on the wrong things."

They found that when you give people more control over their time, the company will get so much more back in terms of engagement and productivity. People in the program were reporting they had a 35 to 41 percent improvement in productivity, and the managers confirmed that it held true.

One group manager was certain the ROWE program would not work for her team. She felt that her people couldn't handle it, and resisted giving it a shot. Cali and Jody talked her into giving it a try, and she started giving more trust and autonomy to her people. It turned out that the bottom performer on the team was now the top performer, and her team was doubling the amount of work they were doing in a month with one less person on the team!

They say the reason for this is that competition shifts from being individually focused to the team being focused on ensuring everyone does the best work. "It becomes natural because everyone is focused on this one thing together; that's where trust builds. We're all using our time the way we want to because we're focused on results. My team supports me and I support them," Jody said.

They both have a strong sense of fulfillment from how this actually turned out, and from being able to do this inside a large Fortune 500 company by sticking to their beliefs. They know the reason people listened to them is because they were saying what everyone was thinking. The people inside the company wanted them to keep going even though they knew it was a tough road.

This was one of the most compelling and interesting of our interviews. These two women were absolutely fearless and had accomplished what many people have only dreamed of. They are challenging the very foundation upon which our work culture is built and shining the light on the absurdities of it. To be able to create change for an organization the size of Best Buy through a grassroots effort, and to transform themselves in the process, is incredible. Now they're on to changing the rest of the world!

Chapter 9

Threads of Clarity

The purpose of life is to live it, to taste and experience to the utmost, to reach out eagerly and without fear for newer and richer experience.

—Eleanor Roosevelt

Getting clarity about what you want in your life and career is foundational to being able carve your own road. As I was writing and thinking about clarity, I thought back to my 20s (I'm in my 40s now), and found the threads of clarity and how they shaped my life.

On a bright summer day in New York City, I was 25 years old and walking around looking for a place to get some breakfast amid the frenetic energy of the city. I felt exhilarated being out in the mix with all the well-dressed, busy professionals on their way to work. Having grown up in the suburbs of Houston, this was a totally new experience for me: In Houston, we were always in a car, driving from point A to point B, and when you primarily get around by car, you really miss a lot!

I was in the city on a business trip at a point in my life when everything felt upside-down. I was in a bad marriage (not to Joe), that I wanted out of but felt stuck in. My dreams had taken a backseat after getting married, and I felt utterly and completely lost. My ex-husband was controlling and emotionally abusive. In his world, my role as a wife was to be there to support him, and not pursue any interests of my own. He wasn't even supportive of me continuing with college, and offered no help in that regard. My parents had to step in and offer to pay for it! I'm not traditional by most standards, especially not being "the wife" who has no say in anything. We had been married for two years and it seemed I had walked into the church with one man and out with another.

As I was walking around that bright morning taking in the energy, sounds, and smells of the city, feeling very alive, everything seemed so vibrant. My feelings were intense; it was as if everything had taken on a new level of depth and detail; all of my senses were overflowing. Out of nowhere, I had a thought, or a thought had me—I'm not sure which.

A loud, powerful voice in my head told me that it was time to live my life on my own terms and start making choices that served *me*. It told me that I had the power to live the life I had envisioned, and it was time to do it *now*; time was of the essence. The voice told me I must take control of my destiny and make tough decisions in order to move my life forward.

It was such a powerful moment, and one that ended up being a major turning point in my life. I couldn't stop thinking about how this voice had come out of nowhere during that moment of exhilaration walking the streets of New York. It was as if the intensity of my feelings and senses had put me in direct communication with my higher self. I felt that I was being guided in order to avoid languishing in a bad marriage at such a young age and missing all the wonderful opportunities life had to offer. It was crystal clear to me that I needed to ask for a divorce. I knew that if I stayed in this marriage, I would end up a bitter woman who always wondered *what if.* When I played out the years in my head, I saw myself as this heartbroken woman at the end of a life filled with regret and missed opportunities. I felt deep in my soul that I was meant to do something big, and I wanted every opportunity to explore what that meant.

———— —

Just two years prior to this experience, I had had a major life-changing event that also gave me a sense of urgency about living the life I want to live "now," and not waiting: My younger brother died of a brain aneurysm. He was just 21 years old and had a full life ahead of him. He was a top athlete, poised to do big things on the world stage, who died on a random Tuesday. It was the most painful moment of my life thus far; I felt as though my heart had been ripped out of my chest. The despair was so deep it's hard to describe. I never got a chance to tell him goodbye or how much I loved and respected him.

However, I learned a valuable lesson from this tragedy: *Life isn't a given.* Every moment we have here should be cherished and lived fully. I had learned in the hardest way possible that your life or that of someone you love could be taken away in an instant. There are a whole series of life lessons I could go into from this one experience...let's just say it shaped me in ways that I never imagined.

It infused me with a sense of urgency to live my life on *my* terms and to experience what I wanted to experience today, not to wait for a "someday" that might never come. My brother had lived his life to the fullest, pushing himself beyond reasonable limits on the diving board, traveling and competing internationally, and caring deeply about what he was doing. He had overcome major challenges in his life to become a top athlete. Many coaches had told him that he was too small to compete and they wouldn't give him a chance. But he never gave up; he turned to diving as a sport and made the decision that he wouldn't be held back by the limitations other people put on him.

I remember him watching videos of himself doing dives from the platform or the springboard. He would watch the same dive over and over again. Watch the dive, rewind, watch it again, rewind again, over and over. At the time, I was annoyed with him, wondering what the hell he was doing. I get it *now*. I get that he was passionate about diving; he wanted to be the best at it and to understand every nuance of his performance. If we all only had something we were that passionate about! Unfortunately, I didn't learn that lesson from him until after he was gone.

I'm glad that I haven't let the tragedy of losing my brother so early eclipse the valuable lessons I've learned from it. He's with me always, and is a constant reminder for me to keep focusing on what I want and living life to the fullest.

— — — — —

Three weeks after returning from my life-changing trip from NYC, I asked for a divorce. Two weeks after that I loaded up a U-Haul trailer and moved to Chicago, a city I had never visited. A friend of mine from high school lived there and needed a roommate, so I decided to make the move. Putting distance between my husband and me seemed the best thing to do, as I wanted to quickly shed my old life and begin a new one.

Luckily for me, my parents have always been wonderful and supportive. They have always believed in me even when my actions didn't quite warrant it. I had made a lot of mistakes up until this point in my life, but my parents were there to help me pick myself up and move forward. My mother didn't want me to move to Chicago and be so far away, but she knew that I felt it was something I needed to do, so she supported my decision. I'm so grateful to both of them for allowing me to make my mistakes, and then to be there for me when I needed help. That's the best parenting there is, if you ask me.

My dad was a great sport and drove the U-Haul and me to Chicago from Houston. We had a great trip together; I remember having engaging conversations about the future, the meaning of life, and the wonder and excitement of moving to a new city. We arrived in Chicago on a bright July afternoon, and the drive up Lakeshore Drive was amazing. There were beautiful buildings on one side of the road, and the massive, brilliant Lake Michigan on the other. The lake looked much more like an ocean to me. I felt so much excitement arriving there; the city was more beautiful than I had imagined.

My dad dropped me off at the apartment and no one was there. Both of my new roommates were flight attendants, and they were out on trips. I spent my first night in Chicago by myself. I barely slept; I laid on the futon in the living room listening to the foreign sounds of the city as fear gripped me. The initial excitement of arriving in the city had worn off, and I realized what I had done. Here I was all alone in a new city, with no job and not very much money. I had left all of my friends and family behind in Houston, and it was going to be completely up to me to make it work somehow.

That year in Chicago ended up being the best and worst year of my life. I was forced way outside my comfort zone on a regular basis. Public transportation was completely new to me, as were many things related to living in an urban city. I remember it being so much more difficult to do the normal things you did to set up your life.

This was change on a major scale. I had left everyone and everything I knew, and was going through a messy divorce at the same time. The experience was like jumping off a cliff, throwing all the pieces of my life into the air and seeing where they fell. I felt exhilarated and freaked out at the same time; I had moments of euphoria and moments of complete and utter despair. I was living at the edge of my emotions.

This was the first time in my life I had lived completely on my own, as I lived at home until I got married at 23. It was pretty scary for me to be on my own in a big city like Chicago, but it gave me an opportunity to live without a safety net and to see what I was really made of. I had to dig deep for my reserves of courage to face new challenges completely out of my comfort zone. Little did I know at the time how important this lesson would be to me and the thread it would have to my future.

A few months later I started to settle in, found a decent job, started dating someone, and had put my life back into some sort of order. I was beginning to relax and feel more in control again. I was feeling more freedom than I had ever felt and was beginning to explore my dreams again. Shedding my old life had opened a world of new possibilities and opportunities I hadn't seen before.

I was working as a manager for a high-end women's boutique on Michigan Avenue. This job was a stepping-stone, because I wasn't entirely sure what I wanted to do, and my opportunities were somewhat limited because I hadn't yet completed my college degree. There was a deep longing inside me to do something big, but I wasn't sure what it was. The move to Chicago had intensified this feeling. Deep down I knew there were steps I needed to take in order to allow my life to unfold.

One day, a man came into the store and gave me his business card. He said he would like to speak with me about a job opportunity he thought I would be perfect for. The job was as a representative for a well-known designer, working the relationship with Neiman Marcus and Saks Fifth Avenue. I was in heaven! That was a total dream job for me at the time. It came with a $10,000 clothing allowance—what 25-year-old woman wouldn't jump at that?

I interviewed for the position, and they made me an offer for more money than I had ever imagined at that point in my life. I was so excited! Then, the other shoe dropped: they asked me for some paperwork, including my college transcripts. I explained that I hadn't quite completed college yet, but could get them what transcripts I did have. He explained to me that the position required a college education, so they rescinded the offer. I was devastated!

My dream job had come and gone so quickly. I went home that afternoon and had a pity party for myself. Then, when I was finished being sad, I made a decision that would prove to be another turning point in my life. I decided I needed to move back to Texas and finish my education, and that needed to be my absolute focus. I would not allow another person to tell me I couldn't do something because I didn't have a college degree. I wanted every opportunity the world had to offer, and I felt that a college degree was a credential I needed to have.

I packed up my meager belongings and moved back to Texas. The drive was a grueling 17 hours, and I cried most of the way. I had grown to love Chicago and my life there, but I knew I was making the right decision for my future. I loved the urban coolness of the city and the energetic vibe that existed there. It made me sad to leave, and I knew moving to Lubbock, Texas, to attend Texas Tech University would be a shock to my system after living in such a thriving metropolis!

Lubbock was indeed a change, but moving there was one of the best and most mature decisions I had made in my life. I knew it was time to focus and get serious about what I wanted out of life, and Lubbock was the perfect place to do that. I had been a very unfocused teenager, and that had continued on into my early 20s. I had dreams, but I didn't have the perseverance or focus to make them a reality. I was a daydreamer who had never fully articulated what I wanted, let alone applied myself in that direction. What I got was a mixed bag of results. There were some good results, and a lot more that weren't so good.

When I arrived in Lubbock, I decided that my focus was to finish school, and I wouldn't allow anything to get in my way. I had two and half years left to complete my degree, and I wanted to get through it in that time frame so I could move on with my life. Being 25 years old at this point, I was ready to get on with it.

Another great thing that came out of moving to Lubbock was that I met Joe. We met one night at a bar (very romantic), but it was love at first sight for both of us. When he walked in the bar that night, everything else faded into the background. He was very cute, and had an air of confidence and brashness I hadn't seen in the guys at Texas Tech. It was the weekend we were playing Texas A&M, one of Tech's biggest rivals. Joe was talking trash to a Texas A&M guy in the bar about the game (the guy was twice his size, but that didn't stop him!). We've been together ever since that night in 1993.

What I've since realized from all of these experiences is that once I decided to get clear about what I wanted and took action in that direction, my life dramatically improved. That was the start of a good life for me, and it is a foundation I built on unwittingly. Now I can clearly see how the threads of all of these experiences have woven together to lead me here.

PART II:

THE MINDSET OF CLARITY PROCESS

Chapter 10

The Mindset of Clarity: An Intro to the Path for Carving Your Own Road

When you are inspired by some great purpose, some extraordinary project, all your thoughts break their bounds. Dormant forces, faculties and talents become alive, and you discover yourself to be a greater person by far than you ever dreamed yourself to be.

—Pantanjali

When you want to make a change in your life, whether it's a career change or just having more control over what you're doing, it's important to understand what it takes to accomplish this. You can't make changes to your life by continuing to do the same things you're already doing every day. Making a big change in your life requires *you* to change from the inside out.

I know this from firsthand experience as well as from the people we interviewed for this book. My life didn't change, even though I wanted it to, until I made changes to how I approached my day. I found that when I began cultivating this practice and applying it systematically, I got movement. By *movement* I mean that things started to happen. Small things at first, and them momentum started to build until my life had changed dramatically within a six-month period.

I had been trying to change my life for seven years since returning from London, playing with different tools and processes I learned from reading books and attending workshops and seminars. I attended more seminars and workshops than I could count, trying to find answers to what would make a meaningful life and how to achieve it. Along the way, I took note of what knowledge and tools were working for me.

Once I had clarity about what I wanted to do and was inspired by a greater purpose, the puzzle pieces I had been working with for a long time suddenly came together. I discovered a process that works amazingly well when applied in a systematic way. I've called this process the Mindset of Clarity because it is about acquiring a mindset that is rooted in clarity. When you achieve this mindset, your ability to break down barriers and get things done dramatically increases.

The Mindset of Clarity process is a framework for not only getting clear about what you really want, but also gaining the tools and techniques for building momentum and achieving your vision by bringing it to life on a daily basis. Rooted in neuroscience and psychology, the Mindset of Clarity process reconnects us to our dreams and the expansive world of opportunity beyond. However, it's important to note that this process is not linear. There is no step-by-step, quick-fix approach.

This process, which is made up of seven different components, is going to help you build a new muscle in your mind—a muscle that creates clarity by feeding off of visualization. Instead of bigger biceps, you're going to create a vision of clarity that opens doors to new opportunities, motivates you to take inspired action, and allows you to connect with the things in your life that create real value.

Building a new muscle is never comfortable or easy at first—the same should be said for this process. The Mindset of Clarity requires a commitment to expand your thinking, put yourself first, and devote a few minutes every day to visualization. It's not a tremendous effort, but this process will become a no-fail part of your day from this moment forward.

If you do this, you will see immediate improvements in your life. They may be small at first, but within weeks, these improvements will be life-altering. Even better, the positive changes in your life will affect everyone around you.

There are seven components to this process—I don't use the word *steps* because it is not a "follow these steps and you're finished" kind of approach. It's about cultivating a practice and a new mindset that will anchor you on a daily basis, helping you to accelerate your vision to becoming reality.

1. Clarity

The first component is clarity. Clarity is the foundation for the process; if you don't know where you're going, it's pretty hard to get there! It's also not an easy step; it takes some deep soul searching and thinking about what you really want. You have to be able to let go of preconceived ideas about who you are and what's possible in order to get to the true core of what you want to create in your life; it's integral to this part of the process.

2. Setting Big Goals

The second component is setting exciting goals. Once you're clear about what you want to create in your life, you need to set some really big, exciting goals to help you move forward every day. When you set goals that are big and exciting, they propel you forward and help you to do the rest of the steps in this process. You will also be setting smaller goals to help you build momentum and get some success on your way to hitting your big goals.

3. Immersion

The third component is immersion: immersing yourself in your vision and goals on a daily basis in a systematic way. This is a powerful process that will help you to connect deeply to your business ideas and vision. You will use tools from sports psychology and the latest brain research to help you build neuronal pathways that will make taking action much easier.

4. Take Inspired Action

The fourth component is taking inspired action. You will take inspired action that is in alignment with your goals and vision. After taking time to do the immersion process in the morning, you will create your action plan for the day.

5. Reflection

The fifth component is reflection: at the end of your day, taking time to reflect on what went well, what you're grateful for, and how far you've come. There is a lot of science behind creating this state of mind just before you go to sleep that shows big benefits for reaching your goals.

6. Evolution

The sixth component is evolution. As you build momentum, you will receive feedback, and it's important to review that feedback and make adjustments. It's also a time to continually evolve your goals and thinking as you hit your goals to keep the momentum moving forward.

7. Letting Go

The seventh component is letting go. This is the hardest part for a lot of people. It's important to trust the process and to trust yourself as you do this. It is about letting go of having specific expectations about how things will show up, and being open to what is showing up in your experience. This state of awareness will help you stay in the flow and enjoy it more.

A Nonlinear Process

One thing that's important to note is that this process is not linear. It's not as though you follow this step and then the next step and then the next one, and you're there and everything is working perfectly. I wish it were that easy!

This process works by helping you to create and cultivate an awareness. Finding clarity about what you want is the first step in the process, because it's also foundational. However, you will revisit this step again and again as you build momentum toward your dreams and goals.

The components of Evolution and Letting Go are also very much about cultivating an awareness and noticing when you need to evolve and expand, or being able to feel when you're in a state of resistance or anxiety and learning to let go. As you become more comfortable in your awareness, you will be able to do this effortlessly.

The components of Immersion, Taking Inspired Action, and Reflection are the daily "doing" components that will help you to be systematic in your practice, giving your vision life and helping you to build momentum. These three components will also help you to stay centered, relieve stress, and allow you to make great decisions and choices that are in alignment with your vision.

When you create a practice in your life that you use on a daily basis, you are laying the groundwork for success.

Chapter 11

First Aspect: Achieving Clarity

Clarity of mind means clarity of passion, too; This is why a great and clear mind loves ardently and sees distinctly what it loves.

—Blaise Pascal

Clarity: What Is It?

The first component of the Mindset of Clarity process is finding clarity. As the title of this process implies, finding clarity about what you want out of life is the foundation for the entire process. Of course, it's a lot easier said than done! It will take deep soul searching and thinking about what you really want. You will have to let go of preconceived ideas about who you are and what's possible in order to get to the true core of what you want to create in your life.

For most people, the notion of clarity is uncharted territory. If you don't believe it, just try answering this "simple" question: What do you want out of your career? It's a tough question. But, if you

127

want to be a successful entrepreneur or corporate trailblazer, then you have to—yes, *have to*—know, feel, and be able to visualize the answer.

Successful people have one trait in common: clarity about what they want out of their careers, what kind of clients they want to work with, and what they want to accomplish. It's that laser focus that helps them determine what actions to take and where to spend their energy on a daily basis. Without clarity, we become distracted. And who could blame us?

Simply put, clarity is what allows you to communicate your vision. Without it, it's hard to answer even the most basic of questions, such as "What does your business do?" and "Why are you in this business?" And, if you can't articulate your vision, why should you expect anyone (customers, partners, investors) to jump on your bandwagon?

There's a certain magical, magnetic quality about people who communicate their vision well. They inspire and attract people— even better, they attract help. People who go about their daily lives vibrantly and vigorously have an energy that demands reciprocation. If you can articulate your vision with passion and conviction, you'll be amazed at how easy it is to enroll people in helping you build your business or buying your offering. That translates into the ability to launch your business faster or move ahead quicker and with greater success.

We interviewed Phillip Chen on our first day of interviews in the Airstream, in Atlanta. He is currently working in a corporate job while launching a business, and is a great example of someone who has taken the time to gain clarity about the type of impact he wanted to have. He created a vision for his life and is now in the process of building the company that will allow him to achieve it. He's the cofounder of HobNob, a company dedicated to helping college students and recent alumni find their life callings.

The vision behind this project is what's driving me; also my passion for it. I decided to sit down and ask myself the question, "Where do I see myself in the future, five years from now or 10 years from now?" From there, I sat down and wrote a vision statement for my life. It's pretty simple, but also lofty. My vision statement is: To be a beacon of light, infusing people with purpose and turning what *could* be into what *will* be.

It took me a while to come up with that statement, and I thought it was really cool. I didn't really know how it would come to fruition. It's interesting to see how it all has come back 360 degrees. I feel like all the pieces are falling into place, and now that vision is what I'm living.

I don't want to be that person who looks back and says, "I wish I had done that." My ultimate goal is of placing a dent in the universe and making a difference in the world. I feel like HobNob will be a great avenue for doing that.

Clarity also helps you evaluate opportunities as they arise to determine if they're worth pursuing. After all, you now know what you want to accomplish, right?

When we're focused, the brain has an amazing power to pick up information and decipher opportunities. For example, have you ever noticed that when you decide you're ready to buy a new car, you begin to see it everywhere?

This isn't a coincidence, as many neuroscientists will agree. When we're totally focused on what we want, amazing things happen. We become hypersensitive to opportunities, strategies, people, and ideas that can help us meet our goals.

As part of our research for the *Carve Your Own Road* book, we've talked to lots of entrepreneurs and successful businesspeople about the path to clarity. Nearly all admitted they needed expert assistance achieving clarity of purpose. Achieving this was key to their success in attracting the right people and resources they needed to launch their businesses, change careers, or just get more control in their lives.

Daryn Kagan was clear about what she didn't want. After finding out that her contract as an anchor for CNN wasn't being renewed, she knew she didn't want to take another anchor role with a news network. She decided to use the experience as a way of reinventing herself.

She knew she didn't want to teach anymore unless I enjoy it

That kick in the butt led me on the journey to create DarynKagan.com. This was the answer to the question, If I could do anything I wanted, what I would I do? DarynKagan.com is a one-stop destination on the Web for inspiring news, and a daily Webcast that features the story of the day. My vision was to have a media company where I owned my own content, so that I know when I do a story, I own it.

The first step was feeling sad and saying goodbye to an old life. And realizing the thing that had defined me for so long is going away. It can be both totally overwhelming and beat you, or you can decide to create a better life. I knew at some point I was going to have to reinvent myself so I figured this was the time to do it.

I didn't know I could be this happy. I loved my job at CNN, don't get me wrong. I appreciate every moment that was…but to wake up every morning and have an eight-second commute to my office and interview inspiring people every day, I feel like I've won the media lottery.

A great way to get clarity about what you want is to spend some uninterrupted time asking yourself some really deep questions about what you want to create in your life. This is so important, because many of us have ideas about what we want, but they are fleeting ideas that aren't fully in focus. When our vision isn't clear, it's hard to know what action to take or where to focus our energy. Once you're clear about what you really want, you want to actively pursue it because you can see and feel what your life would be like with this new clarity.

What Happens If You Don't Do It?

If you're unclear about where you're headed, you will have a scattered approach to life. As a result, it will feel like you're standing still rather than moving forward.

When I realized I was unhappy and unfulfilled in my career, I just knew I wanted out but I wasn't clear about what I wanted. I didn't take the time to get clear, so I took a lot of paths that ended up being detours and dead-ends. I tried many different things because I wanted out of my job so badly that I would try almost anything. I ended up taking a scattered approach, trying to make money without any real thought for what it was that I wanted to create. That just perpetuated my sense of frustration and lack of fulfillment. It's really not about money. It's about doing something that is fulfilling to you and gives meaning to your days. Money is an outcome. We all need money, so I don't want to minimize this, but it can't be what's driving you or you will lose steam once things become difficult.

It's very hard to stay motivated and excited about doing anything when you don't have a clear vision for what you're trying to create and why you want it. It's difficult to make the right decisions and choices when you don't have a compass guiding you.

When the moment of clarity came for me and this framework appeared, everything just took off. It was like all doors opened and people, opportunities, and resources appeared. There is something magical about it when you get it.

How Do You Get It?

Getting clarity about what you want takes a focused approach: sitting down and asking yourself some soul-searching questions and then using your answers to create a vision statement for yourself. The vision statement is about defining the "essence" of what you want to create in your life, and will give you a great starting place.

— — — — —

In this section, we have created some exercises for helping you to gain clarity. The first part is the Clarity Exercise; you can use the one that is best for you. One section of questions is for people who are focused on wanting to start their own businesses, and the second section is for those who are looking for a new job or a career change. The second exercise is about creating your vision statement, and I've included mine as an example.

Clarity Exercise

When doing this exercise it's important to find a time and place where you won't be disturbed for a while so you can focus and immerse yourself in this exercise.

Get a pad of paper and pen, or use your computer, whatever works best for you. It's helpful to put on some ambient music and use headphones so that you can block out extraneous noise and distractions. Writing is a powerful way to focus, and when you add soft music, your experience will be enhanced because you will be able to think clearly without distraction.

When asking yourself these questions, take a moment to close your eyes and picture yourself doing exactly what you would like to be doing in your work life. In this exercise, focus on your ideal career or business that you would like to create—not what you think is realistic based on the economy or what you've heard from other people. Don't define with what you are *willing* to accept, but rather what you want more than anything in your next opportunity.

Go all the way to possibility; don't limit yourself. Go all the way out there; you can always scale it back some. It's better to aim high and fall just short of your goal than to aim for something mediocre and hit that.

Part 1: Gaining Clarity

Here is a short list of questions to get you started.

- Why am I here?
- I lose myself and all sense of time when I
  _____.

- What do I *really* want more than anything?
- What holds me back from getting what I want?
- What am I afraid of with regard to pursuing my dreams?
- If I could do anything I wanted to do and there were absolutely no obstacles, what would it be?

If you want to focus on **starting your own business**, also answer these questions:

- What are my unique skills and abilities that I would like to use on a daily basis?
- What am I passionate about? How can I incorporate that into my work?
- Why do I want to start my own company, what is my primary motivation?
- What experiences can I leverage to launch a business?
- What do I enjoy doing more than anything else in my work?
- What gets me excited and motivated? Remember a time when you were excited and motivated—what was it like?
- What activities do I enjoy that I would like to do more?
- What is my company's culture?
- What does it feel like to be living my dream?
- What is missing from what I'm currently doing that I want to incorporate?
- What values are important to me that I would like to integrate into my business?
- What are my employees, partners, and board members like?
- How does my office or workspace look and feel?
- What is my dream compensation?
- Do I want to build a company, or do I want to be a freelance consultant?
- What kind of growth opportunities do I want?
- What types of things am I told I do well? Do I want to incorporate those in my work?
- What kind of work would I do for free (because I enjoy doing it so much)?
- What type of lifestyle do I envision for myself?

If you want to focus on a **new career**, also answer these questions:

- What are my unique skills and abilities that I would like to use in my work?
- Do I crave having an impact? If so, what does that mean to me?
- What do I enjoy doing more than anything else in my work?
- What gets me excited and motivated?
- What activities do I enjoy doing during the day?
- What types of things am I told I do well?
- What kind of work would I do for free?
- What kind of work/life balance would I like to create (telecommuting, working from home)?
- What is my boss like?
- What are my coworkers like?
- What is the ideal culture and values of my company?
- What am I passionate about? What do I want to do to incorporate that into my work?
- How does it feel to have this opportunity?
- Why do I want this?
- Do I already have a lot of these qualities in my work? If so, what am I really missing?

Lifestyle Questions

These are questions designed to get you thinking about the kind of lifestyle you would like to be living. Have fun with this and really let loose; remember, this is yours to create! Don't hold back because you can't see it happening today; define it as you would like it to be. What's the point otherwise?

- What is my perfect schedule? How would I like to structure my day?

- Do I want a flexible schedule of some sort, working from home, a compressed work week, Fridays off, and so on?

- What would I like to incorporate into my day that I haven't been able to do with my current schedule (exercise, yoga classes, learning a new language, more playtime for myself or with my kids, learning a new sport, meditation, volunteer work, reading, cooking, and so on)?

- Do I want the ability to travel more or take a sabbatical to do something meaningful (spending a month in a villa in Europe during the summer while working remotely, doing mission work for your favorite charity or church, learning a new skill, taking an exotic trip and immersing yourself into a new culture)?

- How do I want to spend time with my family, and how does it feel to have quality time with them?

- How would I like to see myself set up financially? How would I use the money? How does it feel?

Part 2: Creating a Vision Statement

Using the insights you got from the Clarity Exercise, it's now time to write your vision statement. This is about defining the essence of what you want to create in your career, and the lifestyle you want. Your vision statement will be the foundation for this process. You will use it for everything we do going forward.

On the same pad of paper or document, you're going to write down the characteristics and essence of your perfect business, career, and the lifestyle that goes with it. For the purposes of this exercise, skip over the how, where, when, and who, and just stay focused upon the what and the why.

When you talk about what you want and *why* you want it, there's usually less resistance within you than when you talk about what you want and *how you're going to get it*. When you pose questions you don't have answers for, such as *how, where, when,* and *who*—we invite contradictory thoughts into our minds that slow down the creative process. We begin seeing hurdles we don't know how to overcome and that stops us from expanding our possibilities. You can worry about *how* you're going to do it later on in the process.

Many people don't even start something big because they either don't know how to do it or where the money is going to come from. I'm challenging you to let go of the "doing" part of this and focus on creating something big and meaningful. Once you've fully developed the essence of what you want and why you want it, you can begin to explore how to go about taking the action that is needed to make your vision a reality.

If you try to "figure it out" now, you will never get to the point where you've created a vision that is exciting and compelling. It will be a watered-down version that seems somewhat realistic that won't get you very excited. I promise, if you can let go of the normal analytical thought processes, you will be so inspired by what you put on paper that you will want to get moving in that direction immediately!

I assure you, most people thought getting Airstream to donate a $70,000 trailer and sponsor us for this project wasn't realistic. In fact, everyone I told about the idea thought it was a nice dream that would never become a reality. Truthfully, I think most people thought I was crazy. I've learned not to let that bother me too much!

As you go through this process, notice your analytical mind popping in with commentary such as, "How are you going to do this?" "It's not realistic." "Just who do you think you are, anyway?" "This can never work; it's too big." "Can't you just be happy with playing the usual game?" Gently ask your analytical mind to take a backseat during this process, and tell it you will get to those questions at another time. When you begin to notice how your mind works, you can begin to direct it to focus where *you* want to focus.

Write out the essence of what you want to create in your career and life in free form. Write it as if you're feeling it this very minute. The tense is present and the description captures all of your senses. It may be a few paragraphs, a page, or more.

My most recent vision statement:

In my new company, I see myself having an impact. I see myself doing work that has a lot of variety, and I'm out meeting people and doing presentations and spending little time in the office. I see myself building a company; at first it will be just me, and then I envision it growing. My company has a culture that fosters new ideas and creativity, and everyone has an opportunity to try new things and have an impact. I see having a great time with my team and building long-lasting friendships as well. I see our office being very nicely designed, bright and airy…lots of white, great lighting, and furniture. The office has a Zen-like feeling to it, and it's a great place to create and focus. I see the office having an outside courtyard with a lounge chairs and a big family-style table for meetings and lunches.

My business is multifaceted and always evolving. I see myself writing books, having an online business that sells products and services, and an offline business that is centered on seminars and conferences. I see there being many revenue streams, and there are always new and wonderful opportunities popping up all the time to grow the business and expand the vision. I see myself working with and interacting with amazing people who are talented and passionate about what they do and are excited to be a part of what we're doing, and who are really connected to the vision.

I see this company having a major impact on millions of people worldwide. I see my books being published in multiple languages and attracting visitors to our Website globally. I see our message being a beacon of hope for people who want to take ownership of their careers and lives. I see us partnering with many other organizations that are doing amazing things, where there are many complementary opportunities for us to collaborate and work together.

I also see our company developing a corporate giving strategy such that we have an impact on the community locally and globally.

I see myself setting up this business in a way that allows me to set my own schedule. The things that are important to me are time with my husband and family, traveling for pleasure, exercising on a daily basis, eating well, and taking time for creating, meditation, and reflection. I see myself integrating all of these things easily and effortlessly into how I run and manage my business. I see myself setting expectations with the people I work with so they will respect my need to set up my day in a way that is most beneficial for me. I expect to give the same respect to others; my team will have the ability to set their own schedules and structure their work in the way that best suits them.

Financially, I see myself creating wealth beyond my wildest dreams. I see us owning multiple residences: West Coast, East Coast, and Europe. I see myself feeling freedom and peace about our financial independence. I also see myself taking time off between December 15 and February 1, and again from July 1 to August 15 to regenerate, relax, and have fun with family and friends in exotic locations.

I see the business moving toward a model such that we have recurring revenue from products that create value for many people. I feel the luxury of abundance in money, health, happiness, and relationships for myself and all who are associated with this company.

This is just one idea of how to approach this—make it yours!

Chapter 12

Second Aspect: Setting Big Goals

> Whatever you can do or dream you can begin it. Boldness
> has genius, power, and magic in it.
>
> —Johann Wolfgang von Goethe

Now that you've taken the time to get clear about what you want, it's time to set some exciting goals that are in alignment with your vision. It's important to set goals that are exciting to you—the kind of goals that, if you achieved them, it would be a big deal. If you set mundane, run-of-the-mill goals, it will be hard to get excited on a daily basis to do this process and mobilize yourself to take action.

Most of us don't dream big enough; we're taught that most of our dreams aren't realistic and that we should play it small and safe. Our analytical minds will remind us of this over and over again when we try something new. *This* process is for people who want to break free of their fears, excuses, and limitations to achieve results and create what they want in their lives.

When I spoke with Robin Sharma last year about making change and achieving greatness, this is what he had to say:

I believe behind every excuse there is a fear. So if we fight for our excuses, we get to own them for the rest of our lives. **Our passion and desire for our mountaintop, or for whatever we want, has to be bigger than all our excuses.**

Fear is the main thing that holds people back from pursuing their passion. Most of the things we're afraid of happening never happen—fear of change, fear of the unknown, fear of success, fear of failure—and they buy into their fears and stay in their comfort zones. A lifetime goes by, they get to the end of their lives, and they realize they've wasted their life. It's incredibly sad. What would the world look like, what would communities look like, if people understood this information and took their power back?

Success is actually really simple. It's not as complicated as people make it out to be. There are a few fundamentals and common sense, like: don't give up, have a clear picture of what you want, create great value for people, be ethical, and find work that you love to do. Then, just stick to those fundamentals.

There are no extra people on the planet. Every single one of us is meant to do something special. The greatest risk is riskless living; there is no comfort in the comfort zone, there is no safety in the safe harbor, and that's actually the least safe place to be. True security actually resides in being uncomfortable.

This process really started to work for me when I found my Shiny Thing. I had gone through the getting-clear process, and it was clear to me that I really wanted to write a book and travel around the country in the Airstream to interview people.

So, this was the big goal I was very excited about. It was a goal that would be huge for me if it came true. I starting using a process to focus on what I wanted first thing in the morning, before my day got underway. I knew from most of my research that setting your tone first thing in the morning is a powerful way to start your day. I was excited about my goal and I wanted to be focused on it and open for opportunities to take inspired action that would start me on the path toward my goal.

For example, my goals were:

- Write a book about people who had left corporate jobs to become entrepreneurs.
- Get a literary agent to represent us with publishers.
- Talk Airstream into partnering with us on this project so that we could build an interesting platform that would create a buzz and get people excited about the project.
- Travel around the country and interview inspiring entrepreneurs for the book.

These were exciting, stretch goals for me. As I mentioned previously, most people thought getting Airstream to partner with us was pretty far-fetched, but that didn't bother me. A quote I've read over and over that has helped me to push for bigger goals in the last few years is: "Once you make a decision, the universe conspires to make it happen," by Ralph Waldo Emerson.

These were bold goals, and I felt energized and excited when I thought about them. When I talked to people about it, their eyes lit up and it really resonated with people. I had taken the time to get clear about what my goal was, and was communicating it with passion and excitement. For the first time in my life, I was truly inspired to do something big.

I had also heard that it was difficult to find an agent and get a book published as a first-time author. But I didn't let that hold me back from setting that as a goal; I believed in my idea and felt that I *could* enroll a literary agent, a publisher, and Airstream. Nothing was going to stop me!

When you're thinking about setting your goals in alignment with your vision, push yourself to think big—to go beyond where you would normally go. Who knows where it might lead? Many people worry about being disappointed to set big goals and not reach them, so they set goals they think are realistic. I'm telling you, realistic goals are boring, and it will be hard to mobilize yourself—and others—around those kinds of goals.

Robin Wilson, founder and CEO of Robin Wilson Home, was a successful executive recruiter who decided she wanted to take a different path. She set a goal to start her own company focused on home renovation project management: Robin Wilson Home.

Seven years later, she has designed President Bill Clinton's office in Harlem, launched her own eco-design product line called The Nest Store, and was named as a national spokesperson for the Hearst Magazines Home/Shelter Division with titles including *O at Home, House Beautiful, Veranda,* and others. She also regularly appears on *Good Morning America* and the *Today* show. She sets big goals and then focuses on achieving them.

Robin knows a lot about putting in long hours to make her dreams come true; she has definitely put in the time throughout the last few years to see her vision become reality. This is what Robin had to say about following your passion:

> If you want to do your dream, you have to say to yourself, *What would I do if I knew I could not fail?* If you can answer that and truthfully say that's your passion and actually do it, you will wake up every single day, no matter how many hours you've not slept, and all those moments of feeling tired will be overcome because there is this inner fire inside of you. That's truly living.

All of us have the power to achieve our goals and dream big. Many people have forgotten their big dreams and goals, and feel limited by the pace of life, their jobs, and financial and family obligations. It's possible to break free of limitations and get in touch with your dreams and goals and go for them, even if you have many obligations that you can't see past right now.

Gigi Chang is a person we interviewed who inspired us by setting big goals and achieving amazing things. She is the vision behind Plum Organics, an organic baby food company. In her previous career, she led strategic planning at a top marketing and advertising agency where she developed global marketing strategies for Fortune 100 brands.

Upon having her son Cato, she started making organic baby food for him at home. She realized this wasn't typical, and her friends were interested in what she was doing. After spending more time speaking with other parents and doing research into the industry, Gigi found herself inspired to launch in the space. She decided she would offer parents a baby food made from organic ingredients that were flash frozen to lock in freshness and nutrients.

Additionally, she decided that if she were going into this business, she wanted to go big with it. She knew that she had a limited amount of time to launch in the market and make a name for herself and her company. Just a few years later, her products are sold at Whole Foods and Target superstores nationwide!

Gigi's decision to go big with her dream led her to the people, opportunities, and funding she needed. Again, when you make the decision to set a big goal, it's much easier to get people excited and mobilized to help you reach it. Everyone wants to get on board and be a part of it!

Tom Darrow is also a believer in setting big goals. He left his position as director of recruiting for Andersen Consulting in 1999 to start his own recruiting consulting firm, called Talent Connections. The last two years in a row, Talent Connections has been named to the *Inc.* 500 list of fastest-growing privately held companies in the United States. He's built a company of 12 people who all work from home, fulfilling his vision of building a support structure for a team so they could be successful and still have balance in their lives.

Tom continually sets big goals, and knows that even if you don't achieve the exact goal, it's a way of mobilizing yourself and others toward building momentum, breaking down barriers, and finding creative solutions.

When he was elected as the president of the Atlanta chapter of the Society for Human Resource Management (SHRM), he wanted to significantly grow the membership base. There were 1,600 members, and he wanted to set a goal for having 4,000 members within a year. The team thought 1,750 was a good number, but Tom said that just wouldn't get him excited: "Setting the goal for 4,000 members forced us to come up with creative ways to engage people and push the envelope; it gave us the impetus to do big things. Everyone worked really hard and we got a lot of traction quickly. We set a big goal and got everyone engaged; it was quite an effort."

They brought in 1,000 new members that year, which was a record. They didn't reach the goal number, but you can be sure no one was disappointed!

Another key ingredient for setting and achieving big goals is the willingness to take risks and do things that make you uncomfortable. If you want to achieve great things, you must do things you've never done before and put yourself out there in ways that push you to get to the next level. If your goal truly is a big goal, you will have to be willing to embrace this part of yourself in order to accomplish it. The single best way to grow and to achieve your goals is to get out of your safe environment and get into arenas about which you know very little. The more demanding your challenges, and the more pressure and risks you face, the more likely you are to achieve your goals.

Carolyn Kepcher is a great example of someone who exhibited her willingness to take risks and set big goals in her career, and who now is an extremely successful entrepreneur and business celebrity. You may remember her from television, sitting next to Donald Trump on the hit reality show *The Apprentice*. We got the opportunity to meet Carolyn when we were in New York City, and I recently had another opportunity to interview her.

What you may not know about Carolyn is that she started out in the hospitality industry. She interviewed for a position as a director of sales and marketing for a country club in Westchester, New York, not realizing the property had been foreclosed on and was being run by a management company. She got the job, and found that the mission was to get the club ready for operation, to fix it up in order to sell it.

Little did she know at the time she took this job how it would impact her life.

As it turned out, Donald Trump was a prospective buyer for the property, and he came to take a look at it. Carolyn recalls, "I was in my early 20s at the time; I remember when he got out of the car it seemed like he was 9 feet tall! I met with him and we went through the property, and I gave him all the information. He continued to call me over a period of two weeks with a variety of questions. He then called the management company and requested a meeting, and since I was the point person left on the property it was up to me to put together a presentation and present it to Donald. I really wanted to impress Donald Trump and become a part of the Trump organization."

Donald did hire Carolyn into the Trump organization to continue to run sales and marketing for the golf club. Throughout the next two years, she worked under two managers who didn't last more than a year. "When it was time to hire another manager," Carolyn says, "I offered myself up for the role to Donald. He agreed to it, but a little reluctantly, I think, since I was still in my 20s, [and] there weren't many female golf club managers out there. I put together a really strong, trustworthy team. It was very scary at the time, but I'm so glad I took the risk."

After 12 years in the Trump organization, Carolyn decided to take all of her knowledge and experiences and invest in herself by launching her own media company called Carolyn & Co., cofounded with Jen Marr. Their first brand is an online channel and meeting place for women to find answers on career and work/life balance.

I went through my Rolodex, we went out to celebrities, authors, and CEOs, and most were interested in being a part of this community and contributing. It's called Finding What Matters. I've learned a lot from my experiences in the Trump organization and from Donald himself. Don't be afraid to take chances, make quick decisions, and learn from your mistakes. If you want to get ahead inside your corporation, you need to exhibit that you're a person who can make decisions, has new ideas, takes initiative, and is a team builder.

The way I moved up so quickly was that I always had a new goal and continually worked ahead to attain those goals while taking ownership of my work and being willing to take risks.

When setting your goals, ask yourself these questions:

1. Does this goal make me feel excited and alive?
2. Do I feel inspired to take action in relation to this goal?
3. Are my goals in alignment with my inherent strengths and passions?
4. When I talk about this goal with other people, do they also see the vision and get excited for me?
5. Am I stretching myself with this goal, or is it too easy to attain?
6. If I achieved this goal, how would it feel? (You want it to be HUGE, as though you can feel yourself screaming, "YES!!!")

Look at the goal and see if you can make it even bigger and more exciting. One of the reasons it's important to have very exciting goals is that, as you will see in the next step, you will be immersing yourself in them on a daily basis, then taking inspired action. If your goals are mundane and not inspiring, you won't have the impetus to take action. If you do create big goals, this next step will be a lot of fun for you and you will start to see results quickly.

Chapter 13

Third Aspect: Immersion

Imagination is more important than knowledge.

—Albert Einstein

You now understand the power of clarity of vision and the importance of setting goals that are big, bold, and exciting. The next part of the Mindset of Clarity process is immersion. By immersing yourself in your vision and goals on a daily basis for five to 15 minutes, you will be able to connect deeply to them.

You will begin each day by visualizing yourself accomplishing your goals, living your vision, and taking charge of the days, weeks, and months ahead of you. By doing this in a systematic way, you will set the tone for your day, and, in essence, your life. You will become aware of opportunities that you may previously have overlooked. Your interactions with people will become smoother as you will be better able to communicate your clarity of purpose.

In essence, you will be giving life to your vision. That may sound metaphorical, but it's actually true. Science has shown that, during visualization, we are actually paving new neural pathways that stimulate our brains.

The Science Behind It

Top athletes, including Tiger Woods, Mia Hamm, and Lance Armstrong, use imagery or visualization to power their performances. In fact, most athletes use mental practice instinctively and spontaneously on and off the field.

It has long been known that the human mind is a very powerful organ with limitless potential. The oft-quoted saying, "Whatever your mind can conceive, you can achieve," has almost become a cliché. But it was only during the last two decades that modern science has come up with incontrovertible proof that what we merely imagine has exactly the same effect on the body as the actual physical experience.

Researchers have discovered that visualization puts your body through the paces before you physically take action. Vivid images can produce subtle but real firings along the neural pathways that participate in the physical activities you are visualizing.

The key is that your central nervous system does not differentiate between real and imagined events. In essence, sharp mental images, in which all of the senses are involved, are capable of "priming" and "pre-training" the body for a particular activity—whether it's downhill skiing or giving a client presentation. This creates a pathway or connection between mind and body that promotes smoother and more precise physical activity once you actually take the action you visualized.

I had the opportunity to speak with Dr. Kerry Spackman on this topic, a neuroscientist who has helped elite athletes and business executives overcome major performance roadblocks. He's also been recognized as the world leader in training elite Formula One racecar drivers to significantly improve their mental and driving performance, and has written a book called *The Winner's Bible.*

What makes Dr. Spackman and his book unique is that he focuses on lasting change by diving deep into the fundamentals of who we are—such as our psychology, physiology, history, and philosophy. *The Winner's Bible* gives the reader a personalized approach to deliver lasting change.

Here's an excerpt on mental practice from *The Winner's Bible*:

The reason why mental practice works is that parts of your brain will become activated by "mental practice" in the same way as they do with actual "physical practice." We can show this by comparing brain scans of people when they *imagine* doing something and when they *actually* do it.

For example a group of subjects were asked to either:

a) **Imagine** clicking their fingers or

b) To **actually** click their fingers.

Brain scans were performed during these two conditions so the researchers could compare the similarities and differences.... Of course, there has to be *some* difference between mental practice and physical practice, otherwise your fingers would also move during mental practice. As you would expect, the better your mental practice technique is, the greater this overlap will be.

Dr. Spackman also explained that, when he's working with an athlete using mental practice, he has them concentrate on the action and/or skill and the circumstances/environment where the skill is being executed. With a professional person he doesn't necessarily have them focus on training the skill with visualization; instead, he tries to get them to "feel" what it is like to be doing that job, to experience the emotion of the job. This emotion helps drive them to change and give them confidence that they can do it.

Visualization and mental practice are powerful tools. Not only do they prepare you to take action, but they also enhance motivation, one of those critical challenges everyone faces. When you clearly visualize the outcome you want in vivid detail and really feel how it feels, it's hard not to get excited about taking action!

If you do this process consistently for several weeks, you start to see big changes. You will feel the momentum toward what you want, and your day will go more smoothly. You will feel more relaxed and at peace about what you want to achieve.

If you can create a space every morning to do this process, it will change your life! Your days will go more smoothly, your interactions with people will be better, opportunities will show up that are in alignment with your goals, and you will start to feel more momentum.

I suggest you wake up in the morning and jump right into this before you do anything else. The key is to do this process before your mind has had a chance to wake up and start thinking about all the things you need to do today. Right after you awake, you're still in a mild meditative state, and this process works best if you can do it during this time.

If you can't do it first thing in the morning, be sure to carve out some time before your day gets in full swing. It will help you set the tone for your day and create your to-do list. It's important to take the time to control your day before it takes control of you! Be intentional about how you want your day to go rather than reacting to what life throws at you.

You need three things to get started: a pen and paper or your computer, some music that you listen to through headphones, and a space where no one will disturb you for at least five to 15 minutes.

The reason you need a pen and paper or a computer is that you're going to write what you're thinking. Writing is your most powerful way to focus. When you're writing what you're thinking, your brain doesn't have time to wander off in other directions, and you will be able to connect to the deeper part of yourself. In this process, you are going to be using all of your senses, and *immerse* yourself in it.

If you use pen and paper, find a notebook or journal that you can use on a daily basis. It's great to go back and track your progress, so I suggest you keep it in an organized way. If you are creating this on your computer, set up a document specifically for this (you can password protect the document if you want to keep it private).

Listening to music through headphones is a way to minimize distraction and help you focus on what you're doing. It will block out noise in the household, and you can choose music that is inspiring to you. I suggest ambient music with no vocals if possible.

Finding a place where you won't be disturbed for a few minutes is also imperative. It's hard to immerse yourself in anything if you know that at any moment someone could walk in the room and ask you a question or make noise. When that happens, it pulls you out of your immersion and back into your life immediately. It breaks the spell, so to speak. Set expectations with people in your household so that you are not to be disturbed during this time, or get up before everyone else does.

Once you're settled, start writing about what you want to create in your life. I'm going to give you an example from my journal here so you can get the picture.

I feel very good being here. I recognize this time is a powerful way for me to start my day. I am feeling my mastery increase as I do this.

I love the feeling of being in the flow, feeling connected to everything. I love having great interactions with people with whom I come into contact. I realize that I am in control of this; I am the director of my experience. When I realize this, it gives me comfort.

I am very excited about my now and my future. I feel like *Carve Your Own Road* is being fully embraced by Tim Garner at Airstream, and John Willig or some other wonderful literary agent will represent us with publishers. I feel like we will get a nice advance to do this work.

I see us traveling throughout the country meeting and interviewing wonderful people. I see us having a great time learning how to film and create a documentary. I see the press and other shows loving what we are doing and following us intensely. There is a groundswell of support for what we are doing because so many people are wanting a change.

I see my business flowing easily and effortlessly and being able to pay everything off easily and effortlessly. I see my life flowing like a beautiful stream and feeling wonderful.

I am so grateful for so many things. I know that I have a wonderful life and I'm so grateful for it. I love my family and my friends and feel very fortunate to have what I have. I'm also very grateful for Joe; I feel like we are in synch and we are enjoying our relationship very much. I really like it when things are like this. I feel wonderful about it.

I feel myself creating wealth in terms of money and happiness. I feel myself sitting on the veranda of the house we designed, where there is a spectacular view of the ocean, and I am watching the sun set. I feel the warmth of the sun on my face and I'm taking a moment to be grateful for what this place represents and how many wonderful things have happened over the last year.

I feel today being a fantastic day and great news comes my way.

This is actually the first journal entry I did, in December 2006. I think it's important to note that by May 2007, Airstream had agreed to sponsor our project, and John Willig agreed to be our agent in January 2007. Tim Garner told me when I contacted him initially that they get hundreds of proposals similar to mine, but that for some reason he was really interested in this one. I also understand that getting a literary agent is supposed to be difficult, and yet John Willig was the first person I contacted. He came highly recommended, and he's very good, so I feel lucky to have gotten him on board with our project so easily.

This is stream-of-consciousness, focused writing—being focused on what you want to create and achieve while feeling as if it's happening to you now.

If you do this process consistently for several weeks, you start to see big changes. You will feel the momentum of the movement toward what you want, your day will go more smoothly, and you will feel more relaxed and at peace about what you want to achieve.

This process changed my life dramatically and continues to do so. I feel the document I've created is a living, breathing thing, and I'm continually evolving my process and my focus. I've noticed that I've achieved my original goals, so my goals are continually evolving. The key is to get comfortable with the forward momentum and to realize that once you achieve something, new desires will pop up that will take you even further.

— — — — — —

Robin Hensley is a very successful business development coach and president of Raising the Bar. She had a successful career working for Ernst & Young and as a marketing and business development executive for law firms. She had gotten to a point in her career at which she was looking for more fulfillment, and began exploring executive coaching as an avenue.

She decided to try executive coaching and used visualization techniques to help her launch and grow her business. Robin decided to get clear about what kind of clients she wanted to work with, so she looked at her background and asked what she had to offer in terms of real-life success stories. Most of her success was in business development, working with an accounting firm and then in law firms. So she decided the best avenue for her would be to coach attorneys and CPAs that are at the top of their game to help them maximize their rainmaking skills.

During this time she was working in a corporate role, but decided to start building her practice to build momentum before she could make the leap to doing it full-time. She let the people for whom she was working know about her plans so she could do what she needed to do without feeling that it had to be done under the radar. Robin was accustomed to working long hours, and she knew this effort would require her to work during her personal time.

She used visualization and planning to determine what her ideal would be, how many clients she would see a day, what her office looked like, and what revenues she wanted to make. She used a calendar and filled in the appointment times as she would like to have them. She colored the appointments blue until she filled the slot, and then she colored them green. Soon, clients began signing up for times, and her calendar quickly went from blue to green.

She wanted to set her business up for success, and because she was working with highly successful attorneys and CPAs, Robin visualized a professional Class-A executive office where she could work with her clients. She now has an executive office space on the 26th floor of a very nice tower in Atlanta.

Today, Robin is one of the most successful one-on-one coaches in the country. She has continued to grow her business, and now sees 40 individuals in person per week. When she doubled her rates a few years ago, her business also doubled! She continues her success and growth by first getting clear about what it is she wants, using visualization techniques, and then taking the appropriate action.

— — — — —

What if you're still not clear about what you want? How can you use this process to help you?

As I mentioned, getting clear for me was like an excavation process. I had buried my heart's desire so deep I didn't even know what it was or where to find it. As I've been working with people, I've run across many people in the same boat. So, if this is you, you're not alone!

This process can be used to assist you with finding clarity, even if you feel as though you don't know where to start. One of the benefits of doing focused writing and visualization in the morning is that it helps you to continually get clarity about what you want.

Ginny Rand is a speech pathologist who wasn't sure exactly what she wanted to do, but had always seen herself doing something *special* with her life. In spite of this expectation, she had struggled for years searching for that special something. Her most recent career as a speech pathologist involved her in the lives of families and gave her the ability to help children. Even though she enjoyed her work, it still didn't feel like her real passion. Ginny decided to use visualization in combination with writing to discover what she truly wanted to do. Here's what she had to say.

In my daily exercise I began to visualize and write about an overflowing abundance of wealth and freedom. I drew my dream house and mapped out every room, and chose vacations and experiences for my family all over the world. Using all my senses, I explored my visualizations and experienced them in detail. I began to feel a release from the daily work pressures and financial stress I had been feeling. As this progressed, I opened myself to the feelings of having, doing, and being anything I wanted. It was a leap of faith to permit myself to imagine a life so spectacular and so authentic to my true desires. The more permission I allowed my imagination, the more enriched and specific my visualizations were.

One evening, about two months after I had begun this process, I ran into a childhood friend, Catherine, at a cocktail party. Catherine was a divorce lawyer who had shared many of her insights with me over the years. In her profession, Catherine had helped hundreds of women avoid the nastiness and aggression that so many couples fall prey to in divorce, and which devastates the children and leaves the parents bitter and resentful. Catherine's strategy avoids this aggression by teaching women how to use their innate instincts as caretakers and nurturers to manage their husband's emotional volatility in divorce and keep his goodwill intact toward themselves and their children throughout the process.

Her approach is revolutionary in the fight culture of divorce law, where many gentle people are led unwittingly into a battle that is destructive and futile. Current legal trends in property division, alimony, child support, and child custody confirm that Catherine's plan is the best way for women who earn less than their husbands to achieve a fair divorce agreement. Catherine had been wanting to write a book about this for years, but as a founding partner in a law firm, she never had the time.

Later that night, I was home writing on my computer when I had the thought that Catherine and I should coauthor a book describing her insights and strategy for women confronted by divorce. The thought was striking; a rush of energy and alertness kept me running on adrenalin for days. I realized—and I cannot believe now that it had never occurred to me before—that I had everything I needed to do this. I love writing, and I easily found the time to do it. Writing is something I have always received praise for, but I think I took my ability for granted and dismissed it. I hadn't written anything structured in 15 years at the time of this event.

Propelled by the energy surrounding the idea, I began writing that night and finished the book nine months later. With the help of daily intention-setting in my writing and visualization exercise, obstacles that seemed to limit the project vanished, and opportunities and inspired action led the way. In the process, I learned what my true passion was: writing books that help people. I felt a source of renewal and energy in my days that I had never experienced before. I know now that I will always write because of what it gives me.

I will also use daily meditation, writing, and visualization to set my intentions and create my future. This practice has unearthed desires and goals I didn't realize I had. I feel this practice has given me the path to an authentic life, one that uplifts me and inspires me. Without it, I spent most of my time engaged in partially fulfilling activities instead of truly inspired ones.

I now believe that desire is a positive life force, and if we allow ourselves to follow it, expand on it, nurture it, and explore it, it will lead us to our passion and our purpose. I began the writing/visualization process knowing only that I was tired of financial stress and easily drained by most of the work I'd ever done.

By allowing myself to dream, even if the abundance I dreamed of initially seemed selfish and shallow to me, it cleared the way for clarity to enter about who I am and what

I want to do. Intentional writing and visualization continues to be the way I bring my undisciplined mind into alignment with what my heart desires and seeks. Without setting my intention in this way, my choices are only partially fulfilling. When I focus my mind and set my intentions, I am moved by the miracle of possibility that is my life.

Chapter 14

Fourth Aspect:
Taking Inspired Action

The journey of a thousand miles begins with a single step.

—Lao Tzu

Taking action is important in the Mindset of Clarity process, but the action should come from an inspired place based on being in alignment with your vision, goals, and intentions. Once you've achieved clarity about what you want to create in your life and you've started to visualize it and feel it, you will be inspired to take action in that direction.

After you do your immersion exercise in the morning, it's good to take some time to make a list of things to do in the direction of your goals. You will find that if you focus on taking action from this inspired place where you've already visualized it happening, your action will be much easier: You've already paved the way for success by focusing and lining up your energy in the direction of your goals, so any action you take from this point of focus will be well received.

This is the time to set small goals on which you can take action and get results quickly. The goal here is to relax some and try not to "make it happen" through sheer force of action. It's getting in the state of *allowing* it to happen, and recognizing when to take appropriate action and when to be patient and allow things to come into focus. This is a much better way to get things done!

I've read many books about processes, and they seem to leave the action part out of the equation, professing that you can just imagine what you want, and it will show up in your life. There are also books about taking massive action to get results, but most of those don't help the reader to build the foundation of defining what they really want to create from an inspired place.

It's important to have all of the ingredients in place in order to build momentum. The key here is that small steps every day build momentum, and in time it takes you where you've decided you want to go. It's all up to you.

As you start to take action, you will get feedback. For example, I created a book proposal for our agent to send out to the publishing community. When trying to get a nonfiction book published, the process is to submit a book proposal, rather than writing a full manuscript to present to potential publishers. A book proposal is like a business plan for a book, defining the concept and opportunity for the book, how you will market it, who the competition is, and so on.

Our agent sent the original proposal out to numerous publishers he knows personally, and we got feedback. Some feedback was good, some publishers wanted to know more about it, and some couldn't understand it. So we went back to the drawing board with the feedback we received and created a new proposal.

I looked objectively at all the feedback and decided to focus on the changes that I felt were in alignment with my original intent, and I discarded some of the feedback. We went back out for a second round with publishers, and this time we were accepted by a really good one!

When receiving feedback, it's easy to take it personally and get frustrated. It's also easy to start questioning yourself and your idea if people don't go for it immediately. The key is to be objective and look at what's coming in and see where you can make changes that are still in alignment with what you want to do.

Action is the ingredient that gets you out there talking to people, knocking on doors and testing ideas. This is part of the journey, and the feedback loop is part of the process. Focused, applied action that is in alignment with your goals is the key to success.

One of the things I've learned in the last few years is that continually doing things outside of my comfort zone really propelled me forward. I started putting things in my action plan that felt uncomfortable, but I decided to do them anyway. For example, when I started doing research for this book I had identified some key people I wanted to interview. Many of them were already somewhat famous, and had "people" I had to get through to get to them.

I looked at my odds. There was a 33.3 percent chance of a yes, a 33.3 percent chance of a no, and a 33.3 percent chance of being ignored entirely. I also realized that if they said no or ignored me, it wouldn't kill me, and if they said yes, it could be a great opportunity. What amazed me is that 90 percent of the people I contacted responded, and eventually said yes, and many of them I have been able to build great friendships with. If I hadn't stepped outside of my comfort zone, I wouldn't have the opportunities or the new relationships I now have.

I used the immersion process to visualize making the call and getting to yes before I took action, and this really helped. I think my passion and clarity about my vision helped a lot with getting people interested as well. Mental practice also prepared me well for making those calls: I was calm and confident because I had done the call in my mind many times before.

I also realized early on that the other key thing in making calls to enroll people into helping me was to determine how my proposal would benefit them. I looked for ways to create win-win scenarios and let my passion for the project shine through.

There have also been many times when I've made calls and felt stupid because I got tongue-tied and felt unprepared. But there is no substitute for taking action when you're prepared and excited about what you're doing. People really respond and want to be a part of what you're so excited about.

Phillip Chen, cofounder and creator of HobNob, reflected that he was more focused on strategy than on taking action in the beginning of his project. It's easy to get bogged down with the details of a business plan, but there's no substitute for getting out there and knocking on doors, talking to people, and getting people excited about what you're up to.

> I came from a business school environment, where you're supposed to build a formal business plan and a financial model and all these steps before you start taking action on a business. What I now realize is that all that stuff is important, but if you have passion and belief in what you do, it's more important than a business plan. A 40-page business plan is not what it's all about.

> We got sidetracked in the beginning by thinking we had to put everything on paper. I've realized it's more about getting out there and talking to people and understanding who your ultimate clients are going to be. We thought we knew what our business plan was, but once we started talking to people, that original model ended up being completely different than what we had originally thought. I think we should have taken more action and focused less on strategy in the beginning.

When launching a business and/or idea, it's important to commit things to paper and have clarity about it, but be careful not to spend too much time getting all the details just right before taking action. When you get out there and start talking to people about your idea or the vision for what you want to do, it opens up doors and opportunities you may not have thought of.

You'll also get valuable feedback that will help you to determine if you're on the right path. An important note about feedback: You should use your best discretion and intuition when getting feedback. Not everyone will see your idea as a great one and be supportive. Take time to listen internally, and see if the feedback you've gotten is valid or not. You know better than anyone else if you're on the right track.

A sign that you're on the right track is when doors start opening and people start showing up to help you. Daryn Kagan had something great to say about this from her experience launching DarynKagan.com:

> Inspiration comes in pieces; people want this big clump just to land on their desks, and it just doesn't work that way. Collect it as you go, let the pieces build the picture...each piece that shows up is part of the bigger picture, and you have to trust that more is on the way.

> I made it up. I learned as I went. I was off to the races creating and taking action before I even knew how it would work. There's not a dollars-and-cents substitute for passion and coming up with a great idea.

> Don't expect to have all the answers at once. For each thing that shows up, give gratitude. Say thank you, and more shows up. The best resources for me have been the amazing people [who] have shown up. When I don't know how to do something or wonder about a service or a need, I just ask. When you're in tune with something you're passionate about and something that's serving the world and other people, it's amazing the people that show up and help you.

Daryn's online inspirational news channel has been a big success and is continually growing. She also recently authored the book *What's Possible! 50 True Stories of People Who Dared to Dream They Could Make a Difference*. Daryn's story is a positive example of how to carry on and create something amazing when your road takes an unforeseen turn.

— — — — —

I have found that clarity and a profound sense of wanting change are the main ingredients needed to take inspired action. Clarity instills confidence in you and gives you the ability to move forward. This project unfolded for me in that way, and many, if not all of the people we interviewed had that in common. When you have the clarity of purpose and you really want it, you're able to overcome obstacles and be creative about how you're going to get there as well as enrolling others into your cause.

Jodi Weintraub changed her life dramatically by getting clarity and taking inspired action. I've known Jodi for 10 years; she was my boss at two companies and has been a mentor and a cherished friend. I watched her go through this period of her life with awe and amazement at the changes that took place in such a short time frame. In her own words:

> I had a great career in HR and continued to get progressively more responsible jobs in executive management. There were a lot of lucky breaks along the way to go somewhere new and build an HR function where none existed. I loved the front-end creative work of building a new function, and it was a great experience for a while. After several years of doing this I was in my late 30s and had come to the realization that I was doing the same thing over and over again; it never changed. I was also tired of trying to convince people in the organizations I worked why HR mattered.

> I had also come to the realization that if I left my current job, I would just be doing the same thing again at a different company. I had hit a pinnacle professionally and I couldn't stand what I was doing anymore! That was very depressing to me.

> At the time, I was working for a manufacturing company, which was very different than the high-tech companies I had worked at before. I felt very isolated being the only woman on the management team, and I didn't feel connected to my peers.

> Additionally, I hadn't been taking care of myself. I wasn't physically or mentally healthy and had no balance in my life. I wasn't even in a committed relationship because I wasn't happy enough to share my life with someone. I had been so caught up in titles and salary in my career and had lost who

I was in the process. At this point, I really didn't know what would make me happy.

I decided to take care of the physical part first. I had always had a weight problem and I really didn't like how I felt anymore. My life had all the trappings of success but I was disconnected to my own emotions, I stuffed down my emotions with food. Since I had tried a lot of things and nothing had worked, I opted to do gastric bypass surgery. It was a tough road, but as I shed the weight, I felt like I was coming more into alignment—my outside was more reflective of my inside. Losing the weight was the beginning of taking back the control in my life.

After having the surgery, I began to have more realizations about my career. I felt like I could talk a good game, but wasn't sure I could back it up. I felt disconnected from who I was and what value I brought. I didn't feel authentic, and it felt like I was putting on a façade. It was clear I needed to make a change, so after having the surgery I quit my job without having another job lined up.

I wanted to take some time to get clarity about what I wanted in my next role, and I took a Zen Buddhism class. The class helped me to see a few important things about myself. I had stopped living in the present, and the class taught me how to start thinking and focusing on the present rather than the future or the past. I had also been very goal-oriented, wanting to be sure that I got something out of everything I did; the instructor helped me to realize that the important part was the journey, not the destination.

I decided [that] for my next role I wanted it to be client-facing and revenue-generating, rather than someone else's overhead. In the new role I didn't want to be in HR or involved in political games, I wanted to leverage my ability to build relationships. I got clear about what my core skills were and what I enjoyed doing and made the decision [that] I would work on my own terms going forward. My terms were:

confine work to work, not allowing it to infiltrate my life outside of work, and to not do anything at the expense of my personal commitments. I had done that for too long and it was time to take control and have balance in my life.

A few months later I was offered a business development role with a great company. I took the role at a 50-percent pay cut because they were taking a chance on me in an area where I had no experience. It afforded me the opportunity to build new skills in a safe environment while having the balance and time outside of work to build a new life. It was also professionally exciting to see my work generate revenue. It felt awesome to close business; I loved it!

Working in this role at this company, I've had a sense of freedom I've never had before in a corporate environment. My professional life and my personal life have flourished. Once I got grounded and centered, I was able to use all of my skills on my own terms. What's been amazing is that I've been rewarded with several promotions over the last few years and am now the managing director for the Atlanta region. It's wonderful to be able to work on your own terms and still be able to perform and grow professionally.

While making this career change, I knew it was important to also focus on my personal life, and I really wanted to be in a committed relationship. I hadn't been in a relationship in several years, so I started dating slowly again, and met a wonderful man named Glenn. We got married several years ago, and he and my stepdaughter have become a wonderful part of my life!

All of this change happened over the period of one year. I made the decision that I needed a change, got clear about what I wanted, and took action to make it happen. I am continually looking for clarity about what I want in my life, and today I live much more in the present moment. I really appreciate my life and feel like I've come full circle!

Clarity coupled with action yields big results, because when your intentions are in alignment with your actions, it's the path of least resistance. The immersion process will clear the way for you by preparing you mentally for action. This combination is a powerful accelerant, and you will be well on your way before you know it. When you're taking small steps every day in this way, the momentum will get stronger and stronger until you eventually hit the tipping point at which everything comes together.

If you want to create an action plan, do it after you finish the immersion process. It will be very clear to you what action to take after focusing on your vision and what you're trying to create in your life. Try to avoid putting too much on the plan in order to keep from being overwhelmed.

Chapter 15

Fifth Aspect: Reflection

I've found that worry and irritation vanish into thin air the moment I open my mind to the many blessings I possess.

—Dale Carnegie

Using the same tools as the morning Immersion process, a powerful way to end your day is to spend a few minutes with your journal on reflection and expressing gratitude.

This part of the process gives you a mechanism for focusing on what's going right in your life. Most of the time there are many things going well in our lives, but we take them for granted. It's easy to focus on what has not shown up yet rather than how far you've come and seeing the momentum that is happening.

Gratitude is a powerful force in our lives. Scientific studies have proven that people who take this step feel much better about their lives, accomplish their goals, and have overall well-being compared with those who are focused on what's wrong with their lives.

Robert Emmons and Michael McCollough are psychologists who were engaged in a long-term research project generating scientific data on the nature of gratitude, its causes, and its potential consequences for human health and well-being. Religions and philosophies have long embraced gratitude as an indispensable manifestation of virtue, and an integral component of health, wholeness, and well-being. Emmons and McCollough conducted highly focused studies. Here are some highlights from their research:

- In an experimental comparison, those who kept gratitude journals on a weekly basis exercised more regularly, reported fewer negative physical symptoms, felt better about their lives as a whole, and were more optimistic about the upcoming week compared to those who recorded hassles or neutral life events.

- A related benefit was observed in the realm of personal goal attainment: Participants who kept gratitude lists were more likely to have made progress toward important personal goals in a two-month period compared to subjects in the other experimental conditions.

- A daily gratitude intervention (self-guided exercises) with young adults resulted in higher reported levels of the positive states of alertness, enthusiasm, determination, attentiveness, and energy.

- Grateful people report higher levels of positive emotions, life satisfaction, vitality, and optimism, and lower levels of depression and stress. The disposition toward gratitude appears to enhance pleasant feeling states more than it diminishes unpleasant emotions. Grateful people do not deny or ignore the negative aspects of life.

Even if you've had a bad day and don't feel especially grateful, incorporating this step in the evening will put you in a better state of mind and prepare you for a good night's sleep. And we all know that a good night's sleep will prepare you for waking up feeling energized and ready for the next day.

It's also important to reflect on how far you've come. Many of us who set goals focus on the fact that we haven't reached them yet rather than focusing on how much we've accomplished and how far we've come. When you're focused on your goal not being here yet, you set yourself up for frustration and anxiety.

When I added this component to my process, it accelerated things. I've noticed many of the benefits listed from the research project: My energy level is higher, I have an overall sense of well-being, and I exercise regularly. As you can imagine, there are huge benefits to this in terms of achieving goals and just enjoying life in general.

Some evenings I'm not in a grateful mood, but I sit down to do the process anyway (it's especially on these days that we need to do it!). In just a few minutes, I do feel grateful and realize just how wonderful my life is, and there is huge shift in my energy. I'm always amazed at how gratitude opens me up, and any negative emotion or anxiety goes away easily and effortlessly. When we're feeling grateful, it's hard to hold a space for negative emotion.

Here are some examples from my journal:

Good Evening! I want to express my gratitude for a fantastic day! It truly was a wonderful day and my interactions with people were wonderful and I enjoyed it immensely. I am so appreciative of more and more of my days being this way!

I love my life, I'm enjoying myself to the fullest extent, and life feels so very full and vibrant. *Vibrant* is a great way to describe how I feel right now.

I'm so grateful for my new contacts and I'm thrilled to have the opportunity to work with them. I know this is going to be a lot of fun and a good challenge for me. I will have many opportunities to focus and make decisions about where I want to go and what I want to do.

I'm so grateful for the wonderful opportunities that have shown up recently just at the right time. It seems like there are so many wonderful coincidences that are happening that make me feel like I'm on the right path.

I'm also enjoying trying some new things even though I was uncomfortable with them at first, I'm really enjoying that process of expansion and growth.

I'm so grateful for my marriage to Joe; we have so much fun together and I realize how much he means to me and I appreciate his support of me even when I know sometimes he thinks I'm crazy! I also am so grateful for my family and how much fun we have when we're all together; how much we enjoy each other's company and respect each other.

The key is being systematic about this and building your gratitude muscle. Once you get started, you will find more and more things for which to be grateful. When you start to feel grateful for some of the things that you may have deemed "bad" that happened to you in the past—because now you can see the larger benefit of that experience in your life—you know you've built a strong muscle in this area.

Feeling grateful for what you have paves the road for more great things to come in. You will be more attractive to opportunities, and people will want to be around you and help you. You're much more apt to want to help people who have positive energy and who are grateful for what they have rather than someone who complains that they never get what they want.

It's also important during this time to reflect on what's unfolding in your life. Take the time to notice coincidences and synchronicity in your life. When these things show up, it tells you that you're on the right path. The more you notice them, the more they happen. When we are in the flow and on the right path, we experience more synchronous events. The flow of coincidences is our path to higher ground.

Synchronicity can be defined as a non-causal but meaningful relationship between events or states of mind within the human psyche and events in the outside world. More simply, we could call it the experiences of "meaningful coincidence." We have all had experiences that we intuitively recognize as meaningful, though we would be hard pressed to explain them in rational terms. In fact, these "meaningful coincidences" are not coincidences at all but spontaneous realizations of the underlying interconnectedness of all things within the Universe.

—Laurence Boldt, *Tao of Abundance*

The Mindset of Clarity process opens you up to synchronous events in your life. When you have clarity and you're immersing yourself in your vision on a daily basis and taking inspired action, you will attract people and opportunities into your life that are in alignment. When you take the time to reflect, you will see the thread of synchronicity and continue to cultivate the awareness of it in your life, thus opening yourself up for more of it.

Did You Know?

- The scientific literature on happiness and gratitude reveals that happiness yields numerous rewards for the individual and precedes these outcomes— meaning, happiness makes good things happen.

- Negative emotions create a chain reaction in the body—blood vessels constrict, blood pressure rises, and the immune system is weaker.

- When people consciously experience appreciation and gratitude, they can restore the natural rhythms to their body, including enhanced immunity and hormonal balance.

(From, *Thanks! How the New Science of Gratitude Can Make You Happier*, by Robert A. Emmons, PhD.)

Chapter 16

Sixth Aspect: Evolution

Change is the law of life. And those who look only to the past or present are certain to miss the future.

—John F. Kennedy

The Immersion and Reflection processes give your vision momentum, and, to some extent, a life of its own. As this happens, you will receive feedback from inside yourself—and from external sources, such as other people and experiences. It's important to review the feedback and make adjustments based on your intuition. In short, you must allow your vision to evolve.

This is especially important as you achieve your goals. What you will find is that accomplishing one goal usually gives birth to a new one. Each goal achieved opens a whole new world of possibility. One thing you will find as this process shapes your life and you gain focus is that you will begin to reach your milestones more quickly. If you don't continue to build new goals upon the ones you reach, then you stop the flow of energy. Likewise, if you don't allow your current goals to be flexible, you may close the door to opportunity.

It's truly about the journey, not the destination. I know that sounds cliché, but it's true. When I started reaching my goals, I realized that almost immediately a new goal would pop up. My goals have continually evolved throughout the last year and a half in ways I never imagined. When I started this process, my original intent was to write a book and travel around the country with my husband in an Airstream to interview people.

As that dream took place, new goals were starting to take shape. I decided I wanted to build a Website that would be a resource and a community for other like-minded people. As we built the Website I started to see opportunities for products and services that could be delivered through that channel. As I'm creating the vision for these products and services, I'm seeing even more new opportunities.

This process is an evolution, continually growing and expanding your ideas. In fact, it works best when you don't allow yourself to get stagnant. Try new things and ideas in your journal, really allow yourself to expand—stretch yourself. Have fun with it.

Periodically, review your goals and make sure they're flexible. Ask yourself if there is any rigidity in your vision that may be closing off opportunities. If your goals feel constraining, adjust them. And, with the achievement of your goals, create new ones that are bigger and better than before.

One key thing to remember, though, is to celebrate and savor the moment when you do reach your goals—don't just move on to the next one. Take some time to really celebrate, even your small victories. It's the small victories that build the momentum to achieve our goals. And it's enjoying the ride along the way.

During each step along the way, Joe and I took the time to celebrate. When we got the word from Airstream that they were going to sponsor us, I went out and bought a bottle of our favorite champagne and we toasted our success. We have celebratory dinners all the time for our small victories; it makes life richer and keeps you focused on the great things that are going on.

This is not a linear process; it's all happening all the time. You are continually getting clear, taking action, and getting feedback, evolving your ideas and visualizing your goals. This is an organic process that takes a life of its own, and it's important to realize this. As you gain momentum you will continually change and evolve your thinking about what you want; it is a forward movement that is always flowing. That's the beauty of it.

When you embrace this forward momentum and ride the wave of it, you will be amazed at what you can accomplish in relatively short periods of time. Many of the people we spoke to talked about continually exploring and evaluating new opportunities as they arose, and being open to new possibilities rather than shutting themselves off to the flow.

Robin Wilson, founder and CEO of Robin Wilson Home, is a perfect example of someone who has expanded the possibilities for herself and evolved her business in a short period of time. She started out doing home renovation project management several years ago, and just a few years later she designed the *Good Housekeeping* "Greenest House in New York," the *Esquire* "Ultimate Bachelor Apartment," and her new eco-design product line called The Nest. She also held a one-year national spokesperson role for the Hearst Magazines Home/Shelter Division.

Her rule is to say yes first to opportunities. She said that when she would get calls about opportunities, she would say yes to exploring the opportunity before saying no, even if at face value it didn't look as though it was in alignment with her goals. She said this strategy had led to new, exciting opportunities she would never have seen otherwise.

Since launching her business, Robin has made media appearances on all the major news networks and has appeared in *O Magazine*, *O at Home*, and the *Wall Street Journal*, among many others. Today, Robin's mission is to combine healthy living with her passion for design, and her focus is on eco-friendly and eco-healthy products and solutions. Now that's evolution!

Robin is thoroughly enjoying her success right now, and says, "One of the greatest feelings in life is the thought that you have lived the life you want to live—good and bad—your life, shaped by your choices."

I recently had an interesting insight about my life. In my 20s, I was all about figuring out who I was and what I was doing, getting an education and doing the foundational things I needed to do to be successful. In my 30s, I chose the path of making a name for myself in the corporate world and being successful by traditional standards. In my 40s (where I am now), I've decided to completely reinvent who I am and live a life that is completely defined by me. I'm happy about how this has unfolded because the path led here, and I needed to take the steps I took in order to do what I'm doing now. It's an evolutionary process.

For the first time in my life I'm making decisions based on true happiness, and I'm doing something that I believe is meaningful. Life is truly about evolution and expansion, and I imagine that my 50s, 60s, 70s, and 80s will be new chapters as well. I've embraced being uncomfortable and trying new things because it makes me feel alive.

In order to evolve and grow, you have to be willing to get uncomfortable and stretch yourself beyond your limits. If you aren't willing to do this, your life will become stagnant at some point. Change and evolution are always happening around us and it's best to embrace it and go with the flow of it. Most people want to hear that they will get to a place of contentment and just stay there and live happily ever after. Unfortunately, it doesn't work that way.

For example, let's say you have a job that you absolutely love and it's perfect for you. You like your coworkers and the commute is perfect, you have a nice balance in your life, and you feel very content. You've been with this company for three years and you're thoroughly enjoying yourself. You arrive to work on Monday morning and as you're getting prepared for the week ahead, your boss comes into your office and shuts the door. Uh oh...is something wrong?

Your boss proceeds to tell you that the company has been acquired by a European conglomerate and that your department is redundant, so they will likely be doing layoffs. Your position will likely be eliminated even though you've done a stellar job.

Or maybe you've been with a company for 10 years and helped to build it from the ground up. Your role has been very exciting, opening new offices, traveling internationally, and you've felt challenged throughout the years. But for the last year, you feel as though something is missing. You don't feel challenged any longer because the company has gotten big and political. You're not able to have the kind of impact you once had and feel stagnant. It's frustrating because you really liked your job for a long time and the thought of change is daunting to you.

The point here is not to be negative, but that things are *always* changing, whether we want them to or not. Change is the law of life, and if we embrace that, life is much easier. It becomes hard when we entrench ourselves and refuse to let go because we're fearful of the unknown. Evolution in this process is about having this awareness and going with the flow of change, as well as creating change.

Chapter 17

Seventh Aspect: Letting Go

By letting it go, it all gets done. The world is won by those who let it go, but when you try and try, the world is beyond the winning.

—Lao Tzu

This last component is the hardest part for many people. It asks us to let go and trust the process. Most of us are hardwired for control, so this may seem counterintuitive. However, success is not a matter of control. It's a matter of trusting the process, and more importantly, trusting yourself.

It's about letting go of specific expectations about how and when opportunities will arise. You know by now that not everything happens as you plan it—this process doesn't change that. On the other hand, the "letting go" portion of the process teaches us that trying to exert too much control is a form of resisting the natural energy flow that comes from the Mindset of Clarity.

As you go through this process, you will begin to have momentum in the direction you want to go, and that might put pressure on you. That pressure can come in many forms. Some examples are:

- Change occurs in your life in order to support the new things that are coming into your life.
- When you create a lot of momentum, sometimes opportunities show up simultaneously, and that can create a feeling of being overwhelmed.
- Time frames don't always proceed in the way we envision, and that can cause you to feel frustrated and anxious.
- People around you may not understand what you're doing or aren't supportive, and it can put pressure on your relationships.

Trust Yourself

Trust that you are able to achieve your goals and that you are great at what you do. Trust that your vision is a great vision and that you're worthy of it. Many of us don't feel worthy of our goals, especially if they're outside our normal comfort zones. I have moments like that, and I remind myself that everyone who achieved something big started from where I am. It's easy to see other successful people and think that they were always that way and that they never struggled. But those successful people started somewhere, and most of them started at the bottom.

Trust the Process

Trust that following this process will get results. There isn't a perfect way to do this, and as you build your goal-setting muscles, you will be more comfortable with it. What I've put forth are guidelines and some science behind why it works. You can set it up in a way that works for your personality, schedule, and life. Don't try to force it to happen; trust that things will show up, and relax about how and when it happens. Focus on what you want and why you want it, and let go of how and when it will show up.

Trust What Shows Up and Be Open

Many of us have strong ideas about what we want and how it will look. Try to let go of as many of the details as possible and focus on the essence of it. This will allow for more opportunities to come your way. When you are focused on a very specific way that something has to show up, you may not notice an opportunity or resource showing up in a different form. And this different form may actually be even better than what you were imagining. So be open to what's showing up around you, even if at first glance it's not what you expected.

When I first started working with this process, I was very attached to specific outcomes, which made it harder to gain momentum. Recently, I've learned to let go and relax much more, and I've noticed that I'm enjoying myself more, more interesting opportunities are showing up that are in alignment with my goals, and I feel more energized every day.

How Letting Go Opened the Door

The first book proposal for this book was written in January 2007, and we were very excited! We sent it to our agent and then we did some adjustments and changes based on his feedback. I just knew we were going to get a publisher right away; I had done all of my visualization exercises, and I could feel it happening.

One by one that year we got rejections from the publishers to whom John was presenting us. Many people were expressing interest, but we didn't get an offer. We were on the road interviewing people for the book at the time, so I wasn't deterred because I knew we would have a lot more content after our interviews were completed.

After we finished the trips and many of our interviews, I rewrote the book proposal with all the new content. Our agent began presenting it again to a new group of publishers. He was a little slow in getting responses, and he mentioned that there was a glut in the market so the timing may not be right. I was a little frustrated, but I always knew this book would be published.

A couple of months had gone by when I made the decision to let it go for the moment. I knew it would happen when the timing was right with the right publisher. Instead, my focus became building content on the Web and some other related projects. One day, a friend of mine asked me how things were going with the book and I told her we hadn't gotten a publisher yet, but I had let it go for now to focus on some other things.

That same evening, Joe asked me if I had heard anything, and I told him the same thing I had told my friend. Right after our conversation I went to bed, and all of a sudden a new vision for the book unfolded in my head. Chapter after chapter was materializing in my head; it wouldn't stop, so I got up to write it all down in the middle of the night. I was amazed at how it all unfolded in my mind; I could see it perfectly! It was exciting, and I felt good about it and knew it would happen in its own time.

The next day, I got back to the other things I was focusing on and had forgotten about the book again. Four days later, John Willig called to tell me we had a publisher. I hadn't heard from him in two months—I couldn't believe it!

I realized that the moment I had let it go and quit forcing it, it happened. Sometimes we get too attached to what we want and squeeze all the life out of our goal! I will never forget that experience and now I try to be mindful of becoming too attached to what I want to happen!

Joe has a funny way of articulating this idea. He calls it "squeezing the puppy." Puppies are so cute, you just love them and want to hold them all the time, but you can squeeze the life out of something you love by holding on too tight, just like your ideas.

Steps for Letting Go

1. Begin to notice how your body feels when you get into an anxious state of mind. Usually you will feel it in your abdomen, like a knot forming. Become aware of the things that put you into this state and what effects they have on your physiology and your mental

state. Try to observe it happening from an objective viewpoint. It's kind of like getting outside of yourself and watching yourself react to things. Just starting to do this will slow your anxiety down.

2. When you get into this state, gently ask yourself if it's possible to not think about what's causing it right now and to let go of the anxiety, anger, or frustration that is welling up within you from the situation or event.

3. Begin bringing yourself back to a positive mental state by focusing your thoughts on what you want rather than what you don't want to happen or what you fear may happen. About 99 percent of the things we worry about never happen.

4. Ask yourself, if the thing that is causing you anxiety actually happened, what's the worst outcome? Play it out all the way in your mind. You will find that what you're worried about will start to dissipate. It's all about gaining control of your thoughts and where they are leading you.

Here's an example:

You are going about your day and everything is great. You are talking to a friend about your goals and excitement about what you're doing, and she doesn't give you the feedback you want to hear. She says she's heard of people doing what you're trying to do and they haven't been successful, and we're moving into a recession after all. Aren't you nervous about that? How are you going to make money? She's planting the seeds of doubt in your mind.

All of a sudden your great day is beginning to crash, you're feeling anxiety, and you begin questioning if what you're doing is really the right thing after all. It starts your mind into a downward spiral. We've all had this sort of thing happen.

Feel yourself going into the downward mental path and how it affects you physically. Then gently start to bring yourself back to your positive state by watching yourself and moving your thoughts back to what you are focused on. Let go of her fears for you and understand that she meant well and doesn't truly get what you're doing.

You will find yourself feeling better and more positive. Then you will be able to get back to what you were doing before talking with your friend: building momentum in the direction you want to go and focusing on what you want to focus on.

Set Expectations With Others

One of the biggest things I hear from people who are starting a business venture or who are making a big career change is that the people in their lives don't support them. This can be a huge cause of stress, anxiety, and fear. One way to alleviate this or prevent it from happening altogether is to sit down with family members and friends to set expectations and ask for support.

It's much easier to have this conversation once you've gone through the Mindset of Clarity process because you're clear about what you want to do and will be better able to communicate it. Tell them what you want to do and ask for support. Tell them that you understand that they might have fears for you, but tell them you would like to pursue your goal for the next six months and see what happens.

If it is a spouse who is concerned about finances, put him or her at ease by explaining that you're not planning on putting the family in jeopardy, and that you just need some time to flush it out and build some momentum. This will help to alleviate some of the stress moving forward.

If your friends or family members continue to bring up doubts or fears, ask them if they would keep this to themselves for the time being. Tell them that you are excited about what you're doing and would like to focus on the positive aspects at this time, that you understand their fears and doubts, and will take them into consideration, but you're going to move forward for now and explore the opportunity.

People generally mean well, but you don't need to take on the doubts and fears of the world. If you did, you would never do anything! Every entrepreneur I spoke with had to do this at some point with family and friends. You are embarking on something different, and change always makes people feel uncomfortable.

Today, just being in a job is a risky thing because companies get sold, merged, or poorly manage finances, and are continually laying people off. No longer can you go work for a company and assume you will have a job with that company for a long period of time. It's not up to you or your performance any longer; there are many other factors completely outside of your control.

The most important thing you can do for yourself is to create a vision for what you want, focus on it, and learn to disregard your detractors. Many people who've had big ideas have experienced people around them being less than supportive. I've experienced it and Joe has experienced it; it's just part of pushing the envelope.

When Robin Sharma set out to leave his career as an attorney to become an author, he got a lot of feedback from people in his life. Luckily, he didn't listen to his critics and has thus been able to have a huge impact on the world. Here's how he dealt with it:

> A lot of people won't understand your dream and they will tell you it will never work. Anyone who has done anything great has had a healthy disregard for the impossible.
>
> People didn't understand my dream and they criticized me. They asked me: Why would you leave being a lawyer? Why would you call the book "The Monk Who Sold His Ferrari"? Why would you write another self-help book when the world doesn't need another self-help book? What do you know about helping people? You don't have the magic. And on and on....
>
> I overcame that by working really hard on myself. Working on my mind, my body, my emotions, and my spirit. You have to stand for your truth, not the truth of the world around you. The very process of getting the success means you're going to generate a lot of criticism. If you listen to your critics, you'll never do anything great.

Neil Thall has been a mentor to me throughout the last 10 years and has always given great advice. He's also the one who encouraged me to quit my job and start my own company. Without his encouragement and support, I'm not sure if I'd be doing all that I am today. Neil has been very successful in the corporate world as well as being an entrepreneur; he's someone who has truly lived his life on his own terms. Every time I talk to him, he has a new adventure planned, and it seems he's living his life to the fullest. I sat down with him to get his views on this topic, and this is what he had to say:

When I came out of school, the path to success was to be a doctor, lawyer, or professional, so I didn't see any alternatives at the time. What I now realize is that those paths are the least exciting. I've seen many people over the years [who] have taken those paths and have found themselves somewhat unhappy. You have to have guts to be able to buck that system though. The people I know who are really happy have done that. Being really remarkable is following your own path. You will never be successful with something you're not excited about.

I think one of the biggest problems people face is looking externally for approval; when you're following your path it doesn't matter what anyone thinks. I took the prescribed path and did middle-level and then upper-level management and it wasn't fulfilling for me. Four years out of college I started to diverge from that path and was discouraged by my manager from leaving to start my own company. That same manager called me for a job 10 years later!

Chapter 18

Building a Bridge

Only those who will risk going too far can possibly find out how far one can go.

—T.S. Eliot

One way to minimize stress and reduce your risk when making a big change in your life is to build a bridge from where you are to where you want to be, so it won't feel like jumping off a cliff. That's how I did it. Joe, however, jumped off a cliff, and luckily it worked for him and his partners. I think that, for them, there was no other way to do it.

The day I decided to quit my job to start my own company, I had a vision. I was driving in my car, contemplating. I had just met with a client whom I love—Neil Thall, whom I mentioned earlier. As I said in Chapter 2, we were discussing a contract when he looked at me and said, "Jennifer, you don't seem happy to me." That took me aback a little because I wasn't aware that my feelings were so close to the surface. I confessed that I definitely wasn't. He suggested signing a contract with Jennifer Remling, Inc., which ended up being the answer to my dreams.

It was after this meeting that I had my vision of the dark road and the doors opening into infinity. It was amazing! This vision represented making a change. I quit my job on the following Monday.

I will admit I was terrified, but I also felt elated and had a sense of freedom such as I've never felt before! I knew on a deep level that this was the right decision. It felt a little like jumping off a cliff, but I knew that the net would appear and it would work out. The contract with Neil was the bridge I needed. I really believe that when you're in alignment with your dreams and purpose, many doors open to support you. That's been my experience, and every single entrepreneur we interviewed said the same thing.

After resigning my position and starting my recruiting business, I had the mindspace to focus on what I wanted. For the first time in my life, I felt free. I started the recruiting business as a bridge to my dream of writing a book and exploring where that would take me.

It was important for me to have an income, but to also get out of the corporate structure so I could focus on what *I* wanted. In my corporate experience, the jobs I held were all-consuming, and I didn't have anything left for myself. Starting a recruiting business wasn't my dream career, but it was the path of least resistance. Recruiting was something I did well; I had a successful track record in it, so it was easy for me to transition to doing this on my own and keep my income whole. And, best of all, it didn't feel so much like jumping off a cliff!

Building a bridge to your new life is like starting to walk across one before it's finished. After you begin building momentum, you can start walking with confidence and continue building the bridge without worrying as much whether it will hold you and take you to the other side. Taking one step at a time and crossing in your own time in your own way is important.

Building a real bridge is not a one-day task; you do not see bridges going up overnight, and it takes a skilled engineer to master this craft. Bridges can take months, possibly even years to build. It also requires the hands of many, many people.

I find this to be true when building a bridge to your new future as well. It doesn't happen overnight, and it requires the help of many people to get you to the other side. It can be frustrating and exhausting at times, wondering if you're ever going to get there, but it can also be a fun journey, filled with excitement and anticipation of the future and looking back to see how far you've come.

A good example of this for me is planning a trip. We love to travel, and one of my favorite things to do is to *plan* the trip. I thoroughly enjoy the research and looking at all the options of where we'll go and stay, how we'll get there, what we'll do, and, best of all, the food we'll eat! Once the trip is planned, I'm in full anticipation of it. I love the feeling of anticipating a trip; it's almost as much fun as going, and it lasts much longer!

At the moment, we have a trip planned four months from now about which I'm very excited. We're renting a catamaran in the British Virgin Islands with my sister-in-law, Candice, and her husband, Nat. I'm already thinking about our provisions and meal planning, charting our course with the captain, what islands I would like to visit, and how it will feel being out on the water on our own.

In the same way, when you have a future that you're planning for your career, you can feel this same excitement about building your bridge, feeling the anticipation of it, and enjoying the journey along the way. It's much more fun if you're not expecting to get there overnight.

I've been building my bridge for two years, and I'm 90 percent there. I just have a few more planks to put into place, and then I will be firmly planted on my path on the other side.

The first year I was mostly focused on the recruiting business and getting revenue from that in order to sustain myself and have money to invest in the Carve Your Own Road project. A year into it, I got halfway across. I began spending half of my time working on the project and half my time recruiting, which was exciting and frustrating at the same time. I felt energized and excited, losing all sense of time when working on the project. When I had to take time to do recruiting after that burst of energy, it felt painful and heavy.

At one point I was feeling frustrated and angry about having to do the recruiting work; I was in total resistance to it. A friend of mine helped me to reframe how I was thinking about it. The recruiting work was sustaining me and giving me the valuable funds I needed to invest in this other project. I came to realize that, without the recruiting business, this other project wouldn't even exist. That reframing helped me to be grateful for the recruiting business and the valuable role it was playing in helping me to build my bridge.

Today, I spend 80 percent of my time on this project and work related to it, and a small percentage of time on my recruiting business. I feel as though I'm almost to the other side. It's amazing, really: It's been just two years, and doing this kind of work is a complete transformation for me.

I say it's a complete transformation because when I started this project, I had never written anything other than boring corporate documents. I had never had a speaking engagement or built a Website—I had to learn many new skills, build new relationships, and overcome fears I didn't even know I had. I'm quite amazed that it's only taken two years.

Phillip Chen is also in the process of building a bridge. He's currently working for a global consulting company during the day and working on HobNob nights and weekends. Here's what he says about his journey:

> Friends will call and want to hang out, and I realize I can't go because I'm doing a job full time and working on this project at night and on weekends.
>
> It's been a bit of a struggle because I want to quit my day job and just go for it, but the realist in me says not to quit just yet. It's a matter of being patient and diligent right now.
>
> I take pride in doing my job well, and part of me feels guilty...there's always work to do. I could work 60 hours a

week for my job, but instead I'm spending those extra 20 hours of my time on this other project. It's definitely been a challenge, but my passion and vision for it is what keeps me going. I can see the other side and I know I'll get there. I really can't imagine anything else!

Ways to Build Your Bridge

There are many ways to build a bridge, depending on your circumstances, expertise, and financial situation. It's important to take these things into consideration when putting your plan together. The key is to be able to create a way for you to begin moving in the direction of your vision so you can feel the momentum of it. Remember, you don't have to jump off a cliff and risk everything. Using the Mindset of Clarity process in a systematic way will keep you focused on your goals, giving them life and allowing you to take small steps every day, which will build momentum leading to bigger steps and more momentum.

Questions to ask yourself:

- Where am I financially, and what would I need to have in order to be able to focus on my vision full-time?
- In changing my career, will I encounter a situation in which I'm making less money for a period of time, and how will I augment that?
- What will it take and how will I know I'm there?
- What is my threshold for risk? What is my family's threshold for risk?
- What is the path of least resistance for me in building my bridge?

Freelance Work

If you're in a corporate job, a good way to build a bridge is to quit your job and do freelance or contract work in your area of expertise. This can easily be lined up in advance of quitting your job, and I highly recommend that route!

When you work on a freelance basis, you're able to have more control over your time and the freedom to pursue your interests without feeling guilty. You will free yourself up mentally to focus on your vision and take some steps on a daily basis in that direction.

Another benefit to doing this kind of work for me is that I was able to charge more for this type of work than I made at my job, so my revenues helped to fund this project. I needed to build a Website, and pay for travel expenses and PR/marketing support, among many other things. I've been able to pay myself and fund this project through my business.

As I mentioned, recruiting was no longer my passion, but the avenue for driving revenue has been tremendous, and reframing the work in that way really helped.

The hardest part about doing freelance or contract work is that you have to sign long-term contracts or you'll always be doing business development trying to get new contracts. So, this is something to consider.

Stay in Your Current Job, but Set New Boundaries

Another way to build a bridge is to look at your current work situation. If you're in a job where work bleeds into life and you feel that you have no balance, it will be hard for you to focus on another project unless you reframe your current situation. There are many ways to do this, and for most people it takes courage. Once you have clarity about what you want and you've set some big goals, that courage should show up for you because you will be so excited about your vision that you're willing to break down any barriers to getting there. Jody and Cali's story at Best Buy from Chapter 8 is a fantastic example of this.

Many of the people I've spoke with are achievers and top performers, and it's difficult for them to not give their companies 100 or even 150 percent! So, when I recommend doing just that, people look at me like, "I can't do that...."

What I'm recommending is scaling back what you're willing to give to the company you work for a little bit. Here are some ways you can do that:

- Set boundaries around your schedule. Be firm about your evenings being yours and not working on weekends.

- Ask your company for a flexible work arrangement. Work from home a few days a week, or a compressed week. This will allow you to spend less time commuting and also less wasted time at the office doing things like chit-chatting.

- Carve out some time during the week to work on your vision. Maybe it's two hours on Thursday nights and two hours on Sunday afternoon. Let your family know what you're doing and ask them to support you in taking this time for yourself.

- Use this new time you've created to start building momentum on your vision and taking action.

- If you've worked for your company and have been there a long time, maybe you're eligible for a short leave of absence or a sabbatical.

By setting new boundaries and creating some ways for you to have time to focus, you will be able to gain momentum much more quickly. You really do have a choice in this, I promise. If you are an achiever and perform well at work, it is highly likely they will give you some room if you ask for it. Be clear that it will not impact your performance. If your boss doesn't seem open to it, ask for a trial period to give you an opportunity to prove it will work.

Look for a Less Demanding Job

If you're in a job that is very demanding on your time and you can't see a way to minimize that, it might be time to see if there are other opportunities that are less demanding. For example, if you're in a traveling role, look for something that requires less travel. If you're in a high-pressure role, look for a more values-based company. Shop for companies that are focused on balance and value their employees—more and more companies are like this today. The Fortune 500 Best Places to Work list is a good place to start.

Also, many cities have *The Business Chronicle* for their market and they also profile local companies that are great places to work.

The key is setting some criteria you're looking for, and during the interview process assessing the company according to those attributes. The interview process is a two-way street, and you should be interviewing the company as much as they are interviewing you.

Remember, this is a *process*, and it may take some time to get to the other side of your bridge. You will have to make some sacrifices and adjustments in order to create change in your life. If you're diligent and systematic about using the Mindset of Clarity process, you will get results much faster, and the momentum you build will keep you going.

Making some short-term sacrifices and changes in your life in order to live the lifestyle you want to live and spend your days doing what you want to do for the rest of your life is worth it! Keep it in perspective! I agree that change can be painful for a lot of people, but it's more painful to spend your days and weeks and years not living your dream.

I'm living my dream today, and it's continually evolving and growing. I will also admit I still have crappy days here and there. There are days when nothing seems to go right, everyone angers me, and I can't figure out what went wrong. Those days don't go away entirely, but they are few and far between. Most days I get out of bed excited about what the day will bring.

I always wondered if it were really possible to live this way, or if people were just being overly gushy about how perfect their lives were. If someone tells you that every single day is perfect and there are never any challenges or obstacles, then they're not pushing the envelope for new and different experiences. When I'm trying new things and pushing myself, sometimes it's painful, and I wonder why I'm doing what I'm doing. But when I get on the other side of it, it's always worth the short-term pain because I've grown in the process and some new opportunity usually comes out of it.

The best way to live life is to live it on your own terms. We all have that opportunity, we just need to remember it and take ownership of it. It's easy to forget it when we've been so busy doing the things we things we think we should do, have to do, or what everyone else wants us to do. It really is your work. Your life. Your terms. Take back the ownership and enjoy!

Index

About the Authors

Jennifer Remling

Before beginning the Carve Your Own Road project, Jennifer Remling was a corporate recruiting executive for many large corporations. However, after traveling the world and interviewing thousands of interesting people, she realized something was missing. She had become successful by all traditional standards, but she simply wasn't fulfilled—and neither were many of the executives she had recruited throughout the years. Today, Jennifer's passion for understanding the entrepreneurial spirit is helping people redefine how and where they work to achieve career fulfillment on their own terms. A frequent speaker on the topic of professional development, Jennifer has been featured in major media outlets. Jennifer and her husband, Joe, currently live in Atlanta, Georgia.

Joe Remling

Joe has been working in architecture and design for more than 13 years, managing projects that range from residential design to large-scale assembly, including the Georgia Aquarium. He left his corporate architecture role in 2004 to start his own design firm with three other partners after realizing that he wanted to practice design in a way that was more in alignment with the future he envisioned for himself. He has been involved in many award-winning projects, and serves on the board of directors for MODA, the Museum of Design Atlanta, and has been a guest lecturer at The Art Institute of Atlanta, and a guest critic for the Georgia Institute of Technology and Southern Polytechnic University.

Image courtesy of Allison Shirreffs.